Pastoral Leadership

Pastoral Leadership
Best Practices for Church Leaders

Dan R. Ebener

Paulist Press
New York / Mahwah, NJ

Library of Congress Control Number: 2018945517

ISBN 978-0-8091-5378-7 (paperback)
ISBN 978-1-58768-751-8 (e-book)

Published by Paulist Press
997 Macarthur Boulevard
Mahwah, New Jersey 07430
www.paulistpress.com

Printed and bound in the
United States of America

To Fr. Marv Mottet
pastor, mentor, friend

Like St. Francis,
his actions spoke words;
his words spoke actions.

This book finds words from his actions.

Contents

About the Series
Best Practices in Parish Management

"The Church is not a business!" Those of us who are involved in church management hear this comment on a regular basis. The appropriate response is, "Yes, it's true that the Church is not a business. But we do have a stewardship responsibility to use our resources effectively. Frequently, that responsibility requires the utilization of sound business management techniques."

Canon law lists three priestly functions. Priests are responsible for teaching, sanctifying, and governing. Most priests relish their roles as teachers and sanctifiers. But few priests get excited over the parish governance tasks that are their responsibility. Very few men seek ordination because they want to run a small business.

While a parish isn't a business, governing a parish requires a significant number of management skills. Funds must be raised and bills must be paid, presumably under the guidance of a parish budget. Staff must be hired and provided with direction. The significant investment in parish facilities needs to be properly maintained. Church security, regarding both facilities and personnel, has become increasingly important. Parish planning is an on-going requirement. The pastor is expected to show leadership in a variety of areas. The list goes on. And all these activities must be carried out within the constraints posed by both canon and civil laws.

In fact, the task of governing a parish has become even more challenging in recent years. Because of a number of factors, men are often assigned to administer larger and more complex parishes. Some are assigned as pastor of multiple parishes. In some cases, these multiple parishes are a great distance from one another. And in far too many cases, we are asking our priests to live alone.

Unfortunately, our seminaries are so overwhelmed with the educational requirements necessary to turn out priests that they are unable to make room in the curriculum to educate them as pastors. This may not have been a serious concern when the Church was flush with priests and men would spend fifteen to twenty years serving as parochial vicars, in effect serving as apprentices and learning how to govern a parish. But today it is not unusual for a priest to be assigned his first pastorate two or three years after ordination.

The good news is that, in many cases, pastors are assisted by a lay staff. But often the lay staff members themselves lack management training. They too struggle with budgets, managing volunteers, conflict resolution, planning for the future, and other management tasks.

Paulist Press has recognized the need for a series of educational materials to address the needs of church workers, both clergy and staff, who serve in a variety of management roles ranging from parishes to dioceses to social service organizations and who have no previous management experience. The result is this series on Best Practices in Church Management.

This series of books covers a wide range of functional church management areas, presented at a level of understanding intended for those church workers who find themselves with management responsibilities but little or no management education or experience. These are practical guides to parish management, not academic treatises. Jargon has been eliminated. Their purpose is to remove the anxiety from church management. These are the books that could be used in a seminary short course on parish management or presented to a newly appointed pastor. Parish, diocesan, and social service staff members with a background in areas such as theology, education, or social work who have suddenly been thrust into a management role will also find this series useful. Even those with some management background will appreciate the detailed discussions they will find in these books.

I am proud to be working with Paulist Press as the Best Practices in Church Management series editor. Paulist has a well-established reputation for turning out the finest in educational materials to serve the Church. This series is no exception. We have been able to attract national experts in each of a variety of functional management fields to share their wisdom. We hope you will find each book to be an invaluable guide as you carry out your stewardship in service to the Church.

Charles Zech, PhD
Professor Emeritus of Church Management
Villanova University

Foreword

Bishop Thomas Zinkula
Diocese of Davenport, Iowa

Surprising as it may seem, as I was reading this book, Charles Dickens's *A Christmas Carol* came to mind. The author, Dan Ebener, assumed the role of the Ghost of Christmas Past and I was Scrooge, but thankfully without his defining characteristic as a cold-hearted miser who despised Christmas! As we journeyed to my past and revisited my priestly ministry, I saw my exercise of leadership from a fresh, new perspective.

I have served in the leadership roles of pastor, judicial vicar, episcopal vicar, seminary rector, and now diocesan bishop. I have supervised staff, conducted meetings (staff, pastoral council, finance council, etc.), made significant changes (like clustering and merging parishes), done pastoral planning, dealt with conflict (like that associated with reducing the number of Masses), and evaluated seminarians. In hindsight, I recognize that I have done some things fairly well, but in certain cases I could have done better.

It would have been very beneficial to have read a book like *Pastoral Leadership: Best Practices for Church Leaders* prior to my launch into priestly ministry, particularly with respect to the "kingly" role of leadership. I did not learn much about leadership qualities, behaviors, and skills in the seminary. Of course, I did figure out some things along the way by trial and error, observing the leadership of others, and reading about it here and there. But education acquired in that manner is haphazard, piecemeal, and hit or miss.

In this book, Dan Ebener leads the reader on a systematic journey to the heart of parish ministry, taking a look along the way at the challenges parish leaders face in exercising their ministry. Throughout the book, he intersperses useful real-life examples of common leadership situations. In writing this book, Dan brings to bear forty-plus years of teaching and writing about leadership, training clergy and lay leaders, and exercising leadership in the Diocese of Davenport and elsewhere.

In the book, there are aspects of leadership that in one way or another I learned on my own during the course of my ministry, but this book affirmed my lessons, helped me view them from a different vantage point, teased out some nuances, and gave me additional things to think about. For example, in my present role as a new bishop, sometimes people say to me, "Whatever you want/think, Bishop." Dan's advice to resist the temptation to rely on one's positional authority affirms me in my response, "Please tell me if I am about to do something stupid!"

There also are some aspects of leadership of which I was aware, but in certain respects only in a general, somewhat vague sense. This book helped me formally name them, look at them through Dan's magnifying glass, make them my own, and hopefully apply them in my ministry. For example, throughout the book, Dan shares good insights on how to pay better attention, be more self-aware and self-monitoring, listen more carefully and respectfully, ask the right questions, facilitate with greater aplomb, and act more empathetically.

Finally, in reading this book, I learned some relatively new things about leadership. For example, I had never considered that change is at the heart of leadership, that is, if one is not changing something, one is not leading. That is one of the differences between being a manager/administrator and being a leader. Also, I had never really thought much about the fact that disciples are followers of Christ and apostles are leaders for Christ. Disciples are called and apostles are sent. In this book, Dan makes a distinction between "missionary disciples" and "visionary apostles."

When the Ghosts of Christmas Present and Yet to Come take me by the hand to view my leadership now and going forward, hopefully we will see that I exercised my leadership better than in the past because of what I learned from this book as I journeyed with the author through the various dimensions of leadership.

Preface

Welcome to this conversation on leadership. While I may be the messenger, most of the ideas presented here are not mine. They emerged out of dialogue with students, colleagues, and practitioners of leadership from all walks of life. I'm just the guy who kept notes for the past seventeen-plus years, about four hundred pages worth, and crafted them into this book.

This book is part of a series sponsored by Paulist Press and the Villanova University Center for Church Management. It is intended primarily for seminarians, priests, deacons, and lay leaders in a Catholic parish, although the concepts could be applied to any context.

The premise of this book is that the Church needs leadership. John Kotter suggests that most organizations are overmanaged and underled. Many parishes fit this description. (This may sound paradoxical, but leadership and management are not synonymous. In this book, you will find out how different they are). The Church needs more emphasis on leadership—coming from clergy and laity.

Let's be clear: parish management is a critical function. The question is how much of a pastor's time should be devoted to day-to-day management functions. Many pastors would like to become more mission driven and less money driven. We have laypeople with the interest and the expertise to manage the business side of a parish.

The purpose of a parish is to lead people to Christ. This mission should be the focus of every priest, deacon, religious, and layperson in a parish.

Let pastors be pastors. Let them focus more on ministry and less on administration. While the pastor must fulfill his obligation to be ultimately responsible for parish management, he needs to be able to focus on the big picture. Encouraging laypeople to take more responsibility for the day-to-day business operations of parish life would allow the pastor to attend more to the pastoral and leadership challenges in the Church today.

The Church desperately needs leadership. We need clergy who can lead from a position of authority. We need laypeople who can lead without that authority. Leading with authority is no easy task, given the temptation to over-rely on the use of that authority. Leading without authority can happen when laypeople feel passionate about change and begin to influence others to join them.

The purpose of this book is to improve the way we do leadership so that we can become the Church that Christ intended. Research shows that most people leave their bosses, not their jobs. By extension, I would propose that many parishioners leave their pastors, not their parish.

If the Church is to overcome its challenges in this next generation, it will need more leadership coming from multiple directions. Pope Francis believes we are all called to lead in the Church today. The only question is whether we can hear and heed that call.

This book intends to help each reader to unleash the best leadership version of themselves. But first, I have many people to thank.

I am indebted to my students—many of them practitioners of leadership—for the many engaging conversations. Often, I find myself listening and learning right along with them. Then I go home and take notes. Many of those ideas have found their way into this text.

I owe a debt of gratitude to my colleagues for the rigorous and ongoing dialogue about what is leadership, how it works, how we teach it, and what it looks like when practiced with and without authority.

And I owe many of my insights about leadership to the people with whom I have tried to practice leadership, especially those in the Catholic Church, where I have been studying and trying to practice leadership since the 1970s.

Special thanks to these friends: Brother Juan Diego Lavado, OCSO, Dr. David O'Connell, Todd Graff, Fr. Francis Odoom, Michelle Herrington, Fr. Jim Vrba, Barb Arland-Fye, Msgr. James Lang, and Michael Havercamp, for extensive comments on the manuscript, and to Teala Happ, for her help with graphics.

Finally, thank you to Donna Crilly of Paulist Press and Charles Zech of Villanova University for your confidence in inviting me to write this book.

Introduction

A Call to Leadership

Fr. Dave concluded, *"Go and announce the Gospel of the Lord."*

The people replied, *"Thanks be to God."*

The end of each Mass is a beginning. As the people of God, we are welcomed at the beginning of each Mass to "come and see" (John 1:39 and John 1:46) as *disciples*, members and stewards. By the end of the liturgy, we are beckoned to "go...and make disciples" (Matt 28:19; see also Mark 16:15; Luke 14:23) as *apostles*, leaders and evangelists, to love and to serve the world.

The end of each Mass is a call to leadership. We are to go forth to love, serve, and change the world. That is the essence of evangelization. It is an invitation to leadership.

At St. Michael's, where Fr. Dave is pastor, the end of each Mass is an opportunity to visit. As part of their pastoral plan, all parish council members introduce themselves to someone they do not know well. They visit for a few minutes, invite them to the coffee room, and then socialize in the parish hall.

St. Michael's Hall fills up with hearty conversation. People are laughing about the latest edition of children's drawings that are now posted in the hallway. Others are greeting a new refugee family being resettled by the parish. Members of the stewardship commission are bringing in trays full of homemade baked goods and fresh fruit.

A white-haired woman in her eighties, Helen, raises her voice to make an announcement. "It's starting to get cold," she says, "but Earl and I have been thinking about how nice it would be to see a colorful patch of tulips in front of the church next spring. So, we will be here next Saturday morning at 8:00 to plant tulip bulbs. Join us if you can. You can help with the planting. Or just drop off some bulbs if you can't stay."

On Saturday morning, a line of cars and pick-up trucks gathers in front of St. Michael's. As Earl tells it, "Everybody brought tulip bulbs. We planted every one of them."

As it turned out, Helen did not live to see the spring blossoms. She was hospitalized when the tulips began to bloom. However, several parishioners took photos of the colorful tulips, drove two hours, and wall-papered her hospital room with the pictures. After she died, the parish built a large wooden sign dedicating the garden to Helen. The story became the talk of the town.

PEOPLE HUNGER FOR PURPOSE AND CONNECTION.

Many people would love to join a parish like this. They just might not know it yet. Research shows that people long for *purpose* and *connectivity* (Thomas). They want to know they are making a difference on something that matters. They want to be connected to people who are making a difference. People are looking for a lively parish community, whether they know it or not.

The Catholic Church needs leaders like Helen. She demonstrates how leadership can emerge from anywhere. The Church also needs pastors who can encourage parish leadership from among the laity.

We need leadership because we need change. *Leaders produce change.*

What kind of change? Growth in spiritual vitality, stewardship, and evangelization. Joyful celebrations of the liturgy. A deeper sense of lay engagement and participation. More vocations. A radical sense of hospitality. A burning passion for mission. A clearer vision. A balanced approach to charitable outreach and social justice. Dialogue about what matters most.

These are challenges in search of leadership. Challenges seek leaders. Leaders seek challenges. We need more leaders to take up these challenges. That's what this book is about.

Disciples and Apostles

When the Mass ends, the call to "*go forth*" is a call to action. It is a call to discipleship and apostleship. It is a call to follow Jesus and to lead on his behalf.

A disciple is literally *called forth* to follow in the ways of Jesus (Matt 4:19). An apostle is *sent forth* to lead in the ways of Jesus (Matt 28:19). Disciples are followers of Christ. Apostles are leaders for Christ. When we encounter Christ in our lives, he calls us to both.

In the *Joy of the Gospel*, Pope Francis says the people of God must become *missionary disciples*. We must tend to the wounds of society, easing the aches and pains of a secular world that tends toward materialism. We are to reach out to the peripheries, speak with those who are unchurched, visit those who are most vulnerable, and touch those who are on the margins.

WE ARE CALLED TO BE DISCIPLES AND APOSTLES.

As missionary disciples, our *mission* is to enable others to encounter Christ in their lives. As people are transformed by their relationship with Christ, our parishes will grow. Our parish strategies are to foster new life in our parish councils and commissions, becoming the salt and light that transforms people, families, communities, and society.

As visionary apostles, our vision is the kingdom of God. It is a vision of a new Church and a new world, one that we embrace whenever we say the Our Father: to build the kingdom of God "on earth as it is in heaven" (Matt 6:10). This beloved kingdom is the vision that Jesus shares in the Gospels. It is the change that comes from "thy will be done." When we lead that change, we are apostles with a vision for a new Church and a new society.

Some people assume that only those with authority are able to lead. They figure that only those with titles and positions can be leaders. With the Great Commission (Matt 28:19), Jesus calls all disciples to become apostles. He commissions every one of us to lead.

LEADERSHIP IS NOT A POSITION.

IT IS AN ACTIVITY.

Pope Francis believes that everyone can be a leader—pastors and deacons, women and men, young and old, parish council and finance council. Throughout his papacy, he has elevated the role of the laity in the mission of the Church.

Parishes grow more when they rotate people in and out of leadership. When the same people are doing the same thing in the same way for a long time, it is a sign of decline. Vibrant parishes recruit new people into ministry roles and encourage them to take the initiative. These parishes score higher on measures of *engagement*.

Leading *with* or *without* a Position of Authority

This book is part of a series on church management. We will focus on what it takes to *lead* in a Catholic parish. The main theme of this book is that *anyone* can lead change in a parish—with *or* without positional authority. Having formal authority has some obvious advantages with its access to resources and decision-making. Leading without authority also has advantages that will be explored here as well.

In the same way that Jesus was tempted in the desert to use his formal authority (Matt 4:1–11), everyone in the church who has authority—from pastor to parish council president, from deacon to finance council member—will be tempted to use (or abuse) their authority. Those without authority are more likely to step up and lead when and if those in authority take a step back and allow room for others to lead.

Those with positional authority can also choose to lead and not rely solely on their authority. They can lead without using their authority. Leading without authority can achieve more buy-in, motivate more intrinsically, and get longer-lasting results.

LEADERSHIP FROM THE PULPIT…
AND FROM THE PEWS.

Let's say you are a pastor. Resisting the temptation to rely only on your positional authority will be your first challenge to leading change. As a pastor, you can command certain changes. Sometimes it is hard *not* to be heavy-handed because it is easier to *dictate* than to *delegate*. It is easier to *monologue* than *dialogue*. It is easier to *impose* your will than to *discern* the will of God and build consensus around that and the will of the people.

To get leadership results, make the conscious choice to consult, advise, and involve more people in discussing, planning, and deciding the future of your parish. Open your heart, your mind, and your will to discern the guidance of the Holy Spirit (Rom 8:27). What you do as pastor can either encourage or discourage the laypeople to be engaged. If they are overmanaged, or micromanaged, they are less likely to get involved or take any initiative to lead.

The key to leading *with* authority, which can be done, is to resist the temptation to rely on your positional authority. Paradoxically, if you want to lead when you have authority, you need to learn to influence as if you do *not* have authority. When you are using your positional authority, in that moment you might be managing, you might be administering, you might be bullying someone to get what you want, but you are *not* leading.

LEADERSHIP IS A CHOICE.

Let's say you are a layperson. First, you need to resist the notion that only people with formal authority can lead. This is your first challenge. You can lead change without authority. It is your choice whether you lead or not. No one can appoint you a leader. Others can encourage or discourage you. But ultimately, it is your choice whether you lead or not. Like Helen, if you feel passionate about changing something and you begin to influence others to join you in a change effort, you are leading—with *or* without authority.

If you have a position of authority in the church, such as a pastor, deacon, or member of the pastoral staff, you will have the responsibility to lead *and* to manage. As John Kotter teaches, leaders deal with *change* and managers deal with *complexity*. If you are a person in position of authority in the church, you will have to deal with both change and complexity.

If you have managerial responsibility, you may be more inclined to *manage* than to lead. The daily grind of management can make urgent demands on you. It can suck the life out of the best of us. Some of my best friends are pastors who have described managing the parish as the "bane of my existence." The urgent demands of management can inhibit our efforts to lead.

Using the Words *Lead* or *Leader*

The English language allows for some interesting use of the words *lead*, *leader*, and *leadership*.

> In golf, the scoreboard is called a *leaderboard*.

> In baseball, the first batter is called the *leadoff man*. If that person reaches first base and takes a few steps, we call that *taking a lead*.

> In virtually every sport, the captain is assumed to be a *leader*.

> In business, the people at the very top are often called *senior leaders*.

Because I have been studying, teaching, coaching, and writing about leadership since the 1980s, I have become very judicious about the use of the word *leader*. It should indicate more than the biggest, fastest, strongest, best person, or the person at the top.

LET'S BE CAREFUL ABOUT WHO GETS CALLED A *LEADER*.

Using the word *leader* to include everyone who makes their way to the top is a disservice to the whole idea of leadership. It *discourages the practice of leadership!*

The Church and the world desperately need leadership to be practiced by people with *and* without authority. The need for change is all around us. If we see leadership merely as positional, we will wait for leadership instead of practicing it. As Helen demonstrated, leadership can emerge from anywhere—not only from seats of power.

Pastoral leadership is a vocation. Anyone can be called to leadership. It is part of what *Lumen Gentium* called "the universal call to holiness," a phrase quoted by every pope since Vatican II. Recognizing this universal call raises the hope that the challenges of leadership can be embraced by clergy and laity—and that change will happen in the Church and the world.

Distinguishing Leadership from Management

So, what does it mean to be a "leader"? How can we break through the noise of our language and culture that confuses leadership with titles, positions, and those at the top?

When I am asked to conduct leadership retreats, we often begin with an exercise called *concept mapping*. I put them in small groups of four to five people and ask them to draw a picture of leadership *without using words*. It launches great conversations.

Yes, most people begin with the concept of leadership as a position of authority. In churches, people will draw leadership as the pastor, maybe some parish staff, and sometimes the deacon. They place the "leader" at the top or in the center of the picture. Leaders are usually drawn with bright colors, strong muscles, big hearts, huge ears, and loud voices.

LEADERSHIP PROVIDES STRATEGY.

Then I ask them to draw a picture of *management*. The "manager" is also seen as the person at the top, that is, the head honcho. But with managers, the drawings usually include hard lines, squares, rectangles, and arrows that depict flow charts and lines of authority. Gone are the pictures of large ears, hearts, and muscles.

MANAGEMENT PROVIDES STRUCTURE.

The idea of leadership becomes clearer when I ask people to return to their original pictures of leadership and to discuss how leadership is different from management. At this point, lightbulbs go off and many people begin to rethink and redefine their concept of leadership.

Many notice their leadership pictures had smiley faces, mountaintops, finish lines, and sunshine. Those being led are having fun.

Those being managed look grim. They have signs of fear, sadness, or boredom on their faces. They are just going through the motions. The people being managed are often drawn as simple cogs in a wheel.

PARISHES NEED MANAGEMENT *AND* LEADERSHIP.

With further reflection and discussion, participants in this exercise gradually begin to see that leadership is *not* positional. They admit that leaders are not necessarily the biggest and strongest or those at the top. They recognize that leadership can emerge from anywhere.

They also realize that management does *not* have to be all that ugly and foreboding. This process challenges the notion that "leadership is good" and "management is bad." Participants begin to see that leadership and management are both important. Here is how I see it:

Leadership	(1) *strategizes* for change,
	(2) involves a *voluntary* and *interactive* relationship, and
	(3) strives toward a *shared* vision or common goal.
Management	(1) *structures* the order in a workplace,
	(2) involves an *authority* relationship between a boss and direct reports, and
	(3) administers *operational tasks* such as human resources, finance, and technology.

Practicing Leadership and Management

Viewed separately, leadership and management are *necessary but not sufficient*. Viewed together, they offer a full range of activities needed for organizational success. Leaders deliver strategy. Managers develop structure. Leaders promote change. Managers provide security.

Management provides structure in our lives.

Leadership promotes life in our structure.

Someone else can appoint you as a manager. But no one can appoint you as a leader. You can be promoted into a position of authority. But leadership? Leadership is your choice.

Traits, Skills, and Behaviors

Today's popular books, blogs, and articles on leadership herald the "ten essential traits," "six sure-fire behaviors," or "nine required skills" to become a leader. The assumption is that if you develop these ten traits (or qualities), practice these six behaviors, or refine these nine skills, you will be a leader—whether you are *changing* anything or not.

There are many good lists of traits, skills, and behaviors associated with leadership. Most of these lists apply equally to both leadership or management. For example, I might say that leaders are humble (a trait), ask good questions (a skill), and listen (a behavior). However, I could make the case that humility, asking, and listening could equally apply to good managing, teaching, parenting, coaching, or pastoring.

TRAITS, SKILLS, AND BEHAVIORS DESCRIBE BUT DO NOT DEFINE LEADERSHIP.

Managers, teachers, parents, coaches, and pastors can and do practice leadership at times. However, they are not leaders per se. Leadership is not ex officio. We do not engage in leadership activities simply because we hold a title or position.

My Definition

After reading hundreds of definitions, I have gravitated toward the work of two authors, Joseph Rost and Ronald Heifetz, in defining *leadership* as

"a voluntary, interactive process that intends adaptive change."

Leadership begins when you feel passionate about changing something. You invite, influence, and inspire others around you to join you in a change effort. When they begin to join you—voluntarily join you—you are leading!

LEADERS ARE CHANGE AGENTS.

Leadership can be hard to distinguish from *good management*. Both require many of the same qualities such as wisdom, humility, and courage. They require similar behaviors such as motivating, delegating, and building trust. Both require listening, presentation, and other communication skills.

Leadership creates change. Management focuses on the *implementation* of that change. In management, it is clear who the authority figure is. That position does not change from day to day. In leadership, the change agent can rotate at various stages of the change process. However, such rotation becomes more difficult when some members of the team have authority over others.

Leadership gets more complicated when the change agent is a person in a position of authority, especially when that person is charismatic or when others report directly to that person. The tendency is to heap unquestioning loyalty on that person. The higher the authority, the more positive the praise.

I've worked for six bishops and have seen many examples of this. One of my bishops was very extroverted and liked to "think out loud." This worked well with his diocesan team, who knew him well and would challenge his thinking (as he wanted), but occasionally, when he thought out loud at diocesan pastoral council meetings, some people would shut down. They figured the bishop had spoken, and therefore the decision was made.

IT IS MORE DIFFICULT TO LEAD WHEN YOU ARE AT THE TOP.

The more positional power you have, the more tempting it is to rely too heavily on this power because it is much easier to dictate than to dialogue. It is easier to tell than to ask. Leading *with* authority has its advantages and disadvantages. It affords you many resources. But it is a lot trickier. Leadership is *not* dictating the change you want to see.

Whether you are the best player on your soccer team, or the pastor of a church, if you are at the top, the people will most likely proclaim you as a "leader." Just remember that being promoted to a position of authority does *not* make you a leader. You must *choose* leadership.

Words matter. Words frame our reality. They define our meaning. Words used carelessly can change the meaning of a sentence or a headline. If leadership is a core value—and it is for me—then how we define it is more than a scholarly exercise. It is fundamental to my mission in this book. Developing pastoral leaders has become my life's work.

Overview of the Book

Chapter 1 explores the *mindful* and *heartful* ways that we can prepare for leadership. Forming hearts and minds is necessary so we can become human beings fully capable of leading change.

Chapter 2 focuses on the *voluntary* ways that enhance the *engagement* of the laity in a parish. This is particularly important for those trying to lead from a position of authority. Their approach can encourage or discourage lay leadership and lay engagement.

Chapter 3 looks at the *interactive people skills*, such as facilitation, listening, and dialogue, that are necessary to lead in a parish.

Chapter 4 takes us into the world of *adaptive and technical change*. The adaptive challenges are those without easy answers. They require more than a technical fix.

Chapter 5 moves us into the primary role of a parish council, which is *pastoral planning*. We will explore *strategic pastoral planning*, my phrase for a process that incorporates eight steps of strategic planning into the parish process called pastoral planning. We will discuss concepts such as mission, vision, and core values.

Chapter 6 wraps up with the ongoing challenge of developing new leaders as a response to the Great Invitation, which calls us to be *disciples* (followers of Christ), and the Great Commission, which calls us to become *apostles* (leaders for Christ).

References

Ebener, Dan R. *Servant Leadership Models for Your Parish*. Mahwah, NJ: Paulist Press, 2010.

Heifetz, Ronald A. *Leadership without Easy Answers*. Cambridge, MA: Harvard Business School Press, 1994.

Kotter, John P. *Leading Change*. Boston: Harvard Business School Press, 1996.

Pope Francis, *The Joy of the Gospel* (*Evangelii Gaudium*). Rome: Libreria Editrice Vaticana, 2013.

Rost, Joseph C. *Leadership for the Twenty-First Century*. New York: Praeger Publishers, 1991.

Second Vatican Council. Dogmatic Constitution on the Church (*Lumen Gentium*). Rome: Libreria Editrice Vaticana, 1964.

Thomas, Kenneth W. *Intrinsic Motivation at Work: What Really Drives Employee Engagement*. San Francisco, CA: Berrett-Koehler Publishers, 2009.

Chapter 1

Hearts and Minds

Chapter 1 Preview

In this chapter, we will address the following:

- How to prepare our own hearts and minds for leadership
- *Emotional intelligence* and how it works
- The difference between the mind and brain
- How the heart impacts the function of the brain
- How recent brain research informs the practice of leadership
- How to become better stewards of our hearts, minds, and emotions

St. Michael's Parish—Fr. Dave: "How Do I Develop Leadership among My Parishioners?"

Fr. Dave was devoting an hour to eucharistic adoration. He looked forward to this precious time. It afforded him the opportunity for prayerful reflection on his work as a pastor. Only four years removed from seminary, being a pastor presented a new challenge for Fr. Dave. Sometimes the activities of parish life came at him like drinking water from a firehose.

His weekly hour of eucharistic adoration reminded Fr. Dave of the importance of prayer and reflection in his daily life. He knew that taking time to step back and reflect was key to his life as a pastor. It allowed him to become more self-aware of his achievements as well as his shortcomings as a pastor. Being around people all the time was new for Fr. Dave, and these people relied on him to be almost superhuman all the time.

He was beginning to realize just how important it was to develop leadership among his parishioners. There was no way for him to keep up with all the challenges of a parish. The change he wanted to see was much too great for one leader. The secular world was making it more and more difficult to grow a parish these days.

In this chapter, we will explore the importance of prayer, reflection, and self-talk in the practice of leading a parish. The work of Daniel Goleman in the art of *emotional intelligence* will inform our review of this topic. Emotional intelligence has been described as the real difference maker for people working in busy environments.

How well we interact with each other begins with the ability to be aware of our own thoughts, emotions, and actions. The research shows that those who are not *self-aware* are rarely able to be *socially aware* (Goleman). This means that if we don't pay attention to what is going on inside our own hearts and minds, we will not be successful in picking up on what is going on in the hearts and minds of others in our parish.

Moving from Head to Heart

Glenn Smiley was a mentor to Dr. Martin Luther King Jr. When Dr. King first began organizing as a young pastor, he realized he needed help to keep his movement nonviolent. He approached the Fellowship of Reconciliation (FOR), whose mission it is to "create peace through the transformative power of nonviolence." King had studied the nonviolent ways of Jesus and Gandhi. However, he told the FOR leadership that he needed to move *from his head to his heart*. He needed to convert his heart to nonviolence.

The FOR commissioned Glenn Smiley to work with Dr. King. Glenn stayed at Dr. King's side for three years. Dr. King relied on Glenn to ensure that the civil rights movement maintained its core commitment to nonviolence. If you look today at photos of Dr. King and his colleagues being arrested, you will often find Glenn's smiling face among those being carted off to jail.

DR. KING DEVOTED HIS HEART TO NONVIOLENCE.

When I was hired by the FOR in 1979, working out of New York as a young peace activist, Glenn became one of my mentors. What I learned most from Glenn about leadership was this:

1. With Glenn, time seemed to stand still. He always seemed to have time for people. He made a commitment to spend time getting to know people. Glenn loved to tell stories and jokes. He could spend hours telling everyday stories that became lessons for *everyday leadership*.

2. Glenn was usually the *last* person to speak up in a formal meeting. Instead of leading through a charismatic speech to persuade others to agree with him, Glenn would reflect and listen. When he did speak, he summarized the *consensus* in the meeting. He spoke with great clarity as he referred to what everyone else in the room had already said.

To move "from head to heart," as Dr. King put it, is the focus of this chapter. The research shows that when people engage the heart in decision-making, they can make time stand still like Glenn did (Begley). They feel a sense of *solidarity*, which Pope St. John Paul II described as *losing yourself* in the struggle of others. Neurologists teach us that those who engage the heart are among the happiest and healthiest human beings (Begley).

Leadership is a collective activity. It relies on people. Relationships are the stuff of leadership. A congregation is a web of relationships. To practice the people skills needed for leadership, ask yourself this question:

What kind of a human being do I need to become so that I can practice leadership?

As Catholics, we are committed to inner change. Jesus calls us to form our hearts out of his love (Luke 10:27). Ashes during Lent are but one example of how we acknowledge that we are committed to change our hearts, our minds, and ourselves to become better human beings.

LEADERS FORM THEIR HEARTS AND MINDS.

Let's say you are a new pastor like Fr. Dave. Or perhaps you are a deacon, lay leader, or member of a parish staff. Let's say you are trying to change the way the parish council runs its meetings. The first step is to focus on developing yourself to become a better person, someone whose life is centered in prayer and prayerful reflection.

Research shows that we can become *compassionate communicators* by nurturing an inner silence, being fully present to the moment, adopting a more relaxed attitude, speaking briefly, and listening deeply to others (Newburg and Waldman). For Catholics, this entails a rich spiritual life of prayer and reflection on Scripture. Prayer has a powerful effect on the one who prays. It transforms our hearts, minds, and actions.

Leadership is an inside-out activity. It begins with work on the *inside* and moves toward the outside. Most of what is written about leadership is about the *outer practice* of leadership: the skills, behaviors, and logistics of leadership. This chapter focuses on preparing our hearts and minds as the *inner practice* of leadership.

Stewardship of Our Hearts

After three decades of research, James Kouzes and Barry Posner conclude,

> Leadership is an affair of the heart....Leaders are in love with their constituents, their customers and clients, and the mission that they are serving. Leaders make others feel important and are gracious in showing their appreciation. Love is the motivation that energizes leaders to give so much for others. You won't work hard enough to become great if you aren't doing what you love.

The *formation of the heart* is our path to holiness. The *Catechism of the Catholic Church* teaches us to "know, love and serve God with all our hearts." The heart is the place where we can find the quiet of the soul, where we connect with God, and where we develop the capacity to know, love and serve each other—heart to heart—before we can lead each other.

"WERE NOT OUR HEARTS BURNING WITHIN US?" (LUKE 24:32).

The heart is the home where we can *connect* with other people. When the apostles reflected on their experience with Jesus on the road to Emmaus, they said *their hearts were burning* (Luke 24:32).

Neuroscientists now know that the key to happy, healthy, spiritually fulfilling lives is forming the connections between the heart and the brain. When lovers hold hands, the neurological pathways between the heart and the brain are firing on all cylinders. When we actively participate in the Mass, pray the rosary, or spend prayerful time in eucharistic adoration, the same thing happens (Davidson and Begley).

Neuroscientists measure high levels of neural energy between the heart and the brain when people

---

are engaged in prayer, meditation, and worship. Research shows that empathy, charity, kindness, and love can arise in the brain by nurturing the connections between the physical heart and the left side of the prefrontal cortex (Davidson and Begley).

Of course, two thousand years *before* the modern age found this scientific evidence, Jesus was teaching about the *formation of the heart*. He taught, "You shall love the Lord your God with all your heart, and with all your soul, and with all your mind" (Matt 22:37; Mark 12:30), and Luke adds, "and your neighbor as yourself" (Luke 10:27).

Jesus is quoting Deuteronomy 6:5 in this passage. Scripture suggests that the *heart* should be the center, the core, the focus of our lives. "Keep your heart with all vigilance, for from it flow the springs of life" (Proverbs 4:23).

Where is your heart? This is the central question that Jesus asks in his Sermon on the Mount. Is your heart seeking selfish desires, personal satisfaction, and worldly pleasure? Are you seeking a vibrant relationship with God and a loving relationship with family, friends, neighbors, and parishioners? When Jesus asks, "Where is your treasure?" he is really asking, "Where is your heart?" because "For where your treasure is, there your heart will be also" (Matt 6:21).

When we dig deep into our *heart of hearts*, do we find that we are seeking the treasures of this secular world or the treasures of the kingdom? There is worldly competition for the matters of the heart. Plenty of distractions keep us from staying focused *whole-heartedly* on the things of the kingdom. Jesus asks for the entirety of our hearts and minds.

JESUS ASKS, WHERE IS YOUR HEART? (MATT 6:21).

In Matthew 19:16–22, the rich young man was willing to follow all the rules, and live up to all the commandments, but not willing to give up his wealth. He asked Jesus how he could find eternal life. Jesus quickly established that the rich man had obeyed all the commandments, but the man wanted to know what else he needed to do. Jesus told him to go, sell his belongings, give to the poor, and come follow him. The rich man went away saddened. *His heart* was too tied up in *his treasure*.

To know what is in our hearts, we simply ask, *What do we treasure*?

To *lose heart* is to lose the connection between the head and the heart, between our beliefs and our behaviors, between our intentions and our actions. When we begin to lose heart, the only thing left is "hoping against hope" (Rom 4:18), which provides us with hope even when there seems to be no hope. Paul goes on to teach:

> ...knowing that suffering produces endurance, and endurance produces character, and character produces hope, and hope does not disappoint us, because God's love has been poured into our hearts through the Holy Spirit that has been given to us. (Rom 5:3–5)

Tough times call for stronger endurance, which builds virtuous character, which produces hope. This hope can be hope against all hope because God's love *has been poured out into our hearts*.

Neuroscientists refer to this quality as *resilience*. It is one of the six dimensions of healthy brain function for leaders. The other five are a positive outlook, mindful attention, and being self-aware, socially aware, and sensitive to context (Davidson and Begley). Each of them involves a strong connection between the head and the heart.

Scripture teaches us to form our hearts in love, and then to listen to our carefully formed hearts, to be attentive to matters of the heart, to be conscious of what the heart is telling us, and intentional about following the message that the Spirit moves into our hearts. If we are to discern the will of the Spirit and follow the ways of the Spirit, we are to set our hearts and minds on nothing but the Spirit (Rom 8:5).

Pastoral Leadership: Best Practices for Church Leaders

Take the case of Mary Magdalen at the foot of the cross (John 19:25). All four Gospels name her as staying with Jesus throughout the Crucifixion, even when all hope seemed gone. Matthew also describes her as being "there, sitting opposite the tomb" (Matt 27:61). No wonder she is the first one to witness the Resurrection (Matt 28; Mark 16; Luke 24; John 20). Maybe she stood vigil from Good Friday to Easter Sunday. What faith! What hope!

Mary Magdalen's ability to hope against all hope is a witness to the resilience critical to leadership. As parish leaders, we need to be aware of how powerful the heart is—and how the action of the heart can change the function of the brain. The heart nurtures *empathy*. This is counterintuitive for the brain. Empathy is a choice made in the heart. It is the basis for *heartful leadership*.

Brain Function

Let's look at four sections of the brain most critical to our conversation about leadership:

1. The *amygdala* is the deepest section of the limbic system. It is designed for human protection and security, that is, for flight or fight. It has a back-alley neurological connection that allows us to act instantly and instinctively. It governs our sensory motor and survival instincts. It can signal an instant hormonal reaction to a perceived threat.

2. The *limbic* system is our emotional center. Every physical sensation goes through the limbic system before it reaches the cognitive sections of the brain. This means that every thought has an emotion tied to it—even before we become consciously aware of the thought. It can trigger physiological reactions in blood flow to the heart and muscles.

3. The *neocortex* is the largest part of the brain. It is the seat of cognition, where our thoughts and ideas are formed. Most of us never use enough of this part of the brain. It processes data, governs language, and allows for critical thinking.

4. The *prefrontal cortex* is a key center for the neocortex. Not all brain activity reaches this area. It is where decisions can be processed. It allows us to think about our thoughts, to be aware of our emotions, and to be conscious of our behaviors. This is where some say that the mind can enter into brain function.

There is a hierarchy here. The brain automatically defers to the amygdala when we have not developed capacity in the neocortex. The amygdala operates only on the present moment. The rest of the limbic system can consider the past and the present to form emotions. It is only when the brain function reaches the neocortex, and especially in the prefrontal lobes, that the brain fully considers the past, present, and future.

When we pray, neuroscientists can measure the neural connectivity of the heart to the left side of our prefrontal cortex (PFC). When Fr. Dave was engaged in eucharistic adoration, he was literally strengthening the neurological pathways between his head and his heart. Whenever we take time to prayerfully think about our past and present thoughts, and quietly scan our past and present emotions, silently reflect on our own thoughts, and consider what we would do in the future, we are connecting the head and the heart. In the process, we are becoming a more compassionate, loving, and caring human being—and preparing for leadership!

PRAYER STRENGTHENS THE CONNECTIONS TO THE HEART.

When we engage the heart, we involve the parasympathetic nervous system in our body. During eucharistic adoration, Fr. Dave was literally "softening" his view of himself and other people. He was lowering his blood pressure, relaxing his muscles, and striking a health balance in his body. Like a deer path in the woods, when we walk that pathway between the heart and the head (specifically, the PFC), we become more and more likely to use that path.

Some neuroscientists even suggest that the heart is another section of the brain!

The Psalmist tells us, "O that today you would listen to his voice! Do not harden your hearts" (Ps 95:7–8). What does it mean to "harden" our hearts? Perhaps it means to "carry a grudge" or "harbor a resentment." Think about those two metaphors. How healthy does it sound to "carry" a grudge? What does it do to us when we "harbor" a resentment? Instead, prayer and reflection can *soften* our hearts. Literally. They activate the parasympathetic systems and strengthen the neurological pathways to the heart.

To harden your heart is not healthy for neither your physical heart nor your spiritual life. Instead, think of how we can lighten our load when we give ourselves *positive self-talk*, soften our hearts, and give others the benefit of the doubt.

POSITIVE SELF-TALK CHANGES OUR NEUROLOGY.

Self-talk is the voice of the mind over the power of the brain. With positive self-talk, we can change the way we think, feel, and act. We can form a more *positive outlook* (Davidson and Begley).

Let's say that you and Bob are greeters for the 9:00 a.m. Mass. You have one door and Bob has the other. However, Bob does not show up for Mass until 9:02 a.m. The Mass has already started, so you can't talk to Bob about what happened. If you assume the worst and start telling yourself that Bob is lazy, irresponsible, and egotistic, it can change your relationship with Bob. When you think the worst, it also has a negative impact on your own mind, body, and spirit. You develop a negative outlook.

Instead, positive self-talk can produce different results. Imagine if you think positive thoughts about Bob. Perhaps he had some medical emergency in his family. Maybe something happened on his way to church. What if he was a Good Samaritan and stopped to help someone on his way to church? Thinking the best about Bob will give you positive energy during the Mass and strengthen your relationship with Bob. It also improves your heart and brain function.

ENGAGING THE HEART CHANGES THE FUNCTION OF THE BRAIN.

Research on Tibetan monks such as the Dalai Lama demonstrates that years of compassion meditation have built strong neurological pathways between their brains and hearts (Begley). This research shows that the yogis' minds can very quickly shift their attention away from the autonomic reactions of the amygdala. For these monks, stimuli from the senses can engage the heart and reach the prefrontal cortex *within milliseconds*, whereas for most of us, it takes at least six seconds.

Pastoral Leadership: Best Practices for Church Leaders

Remember that when sensations are sent from any of the five senses to the brain, they must travel through the emotional (limbic) center of the brain before the sensation is processed by the neocortex, which includes the prefrontal cortex. This means that our thoughts and words are heavily influenced by emotional ties to every stimulus.

Negative emotions such as fear, anger, and anxiety can cause a rough time on our thoughts, intentions, and behaviors. The hormones they release can make it difficult to pay close attention to what else is happening in the room. We immediately become less centered, less still, and less focused on the present moment.

Unless we pause long enough to allow the brain activity to move all the way to the prefrontal cortex, and then to connect to the heart, we might make a lot of selfish decisions.

Reflection Question:

What are the distractions that keep you from living fully in the present moment?

Heartful Leadership

Think about the parable of the Good Samaritan (Luke 10:25–37). The mindset of the priest and the Levite was, *"If I stop to help this person, what will happen to me?"* This question is based on fear. The brain activity is signaling fear that the man on the side of the road could have been setting a trap. When the brain senses fear, the body is inclined to run away.

Imagine you are walking in the woods. You are about to bump your head into a branch. Your immediate response is to duck your head. You might not even be aware you did it. Imagine you are driving and you suddenly swerve so you don't hit a child. These are immediate reactions. The amygdala is designed for these quick responses to potential danger.

THE GOOD SAMARITAN REPLIED WITH HIS HEART.

On the other hand, the mindset of the Good Samaritan was to reverse the question: *"If I do not stop to help this person, what will happen to him?"* This is the question that Martin Luther King Jr asked himself in his famous sermon he gave the night before he died: *If he did not stop to help the sanitation workers in Memphis, what would happen to them?* To enter into this type of thinking requires processing the brain activity all the way from the amygdala to the prefrontal cortex—and to the heart. The response of the Good Samaritan is *from the heart*.

Two thousand years before the neuroscientists conducted research showing the heart and the brain were so well connected, Jesus taught us to listen to the voice of our hearts. The heart speaks to us only if we are willing and able to listen. As the Anglican Book of Common Prayer puts it, "Cleanse the thoughts of our hearts by the inspiration of thy Holy Spirit."

I would like to believe these scientists are right: perhaps the heart is another section of the brain. The distance from head to heart is said to be about eighteen inches. But that eighteen-inch journey is more than a physical path from a nerve center to a blood pump. It is a spiritual path to God. It is a spiritual journey to the heart. Some say it is the longest distance in the world. It is the journey for *heartful leadership*.

Discussion Questions

What is the heart?

What does it mean to take heart, or to have a big heart?

What is heartfelt thanks?

What does it mean to speak from the heart?

What do we mean when we say that something or someone breaks our heart?

Stewardship of the Mind

What is the difference between the brain and the mind? Is the brain the seat and source of the mind or is it the other way around? This has been a long debate in science.

Recent research has changed the way science views the brain. In the past, scientists believed that we are born with all the neurons we are ever going to have. Supposedly, most of our intelligence, disposition, and mental health was determined at birth. That is now considered an old idea in medical science.

THE MIND CAN ALSO CHANGE THE FUNCTION OF THE BRAIN.

The human brain runs in patterns. Billions of neurons form trillions of connections that are always changing and adapting to our sensations, choices, and experiences.

Science now teaches that the adult brain generates new neurons instead of just rearranging the neurons it already has. This is called the *neuroplasticity* of the brain, its ability to reorganize itself, to change and grow. Activities that stimulate the growth of new neurons include physical activities like walking in the woods, eating the right foods, and presenting yourself to positive self-talk. It also includes prayer, meditation, and worship!

The conscious act of thinking about our thoughts, the willful feat of changing the way we think, the intentional practice of being more aware of the patterns of the brain, the spiritual exercise of saying the rosary—all of this can change the neurological activities and structural connections of the brain. The more we are awake to this reality, the more we can have a positive, proactive impact by calibrating the growth and development of our brain!

Where does this conscious energy emerge from? It is what we call *the mind*. The mind is that innate voice, that *free will* that allows us to make conscious choices, to be aware of the habits of our thoughts and emotions, to practice restraint before acting. It is what we call mind over matter, or more aptly, ***mind over brain***.

The mind, it now appears, has more control of the brain than vice versa. In fact, scientists now recognize the power of the mind to *transform the brain*.

As leaders, sometimes we need to *think* about what we really see so that we can *see* what we really think. It is what Ronald Heifetz would describe as "getting on the balcony" to see our inner actions, our interactions, and ourselves from afar. It is what Otto Scharmer describes as "presencing," being awake to the here and now so we can see from the deepest source of wisdom.

Our mind allows us to be fully aware of our thoughts, emotions, and behaviors. However, the hyperactive pace of our lives, the constant stimulation, the multitasking, and the multitude of distractions we are receiving from many directions make it extremely difficult to employ the full power of mind over brain in our daily lives.

Pastoral Leadership: Best Practices for Church Leaders

Mindful Leadership

Mindfulness is the word we use to describe this power to think about our thoughts and redirect our thinking toward something more positive. Mindfulness helps us to capture the moment, to be aware of our sensations and conscious of our feelings. It invites us to awaken mindfully, walk mindfully, pray mindfully, pause mindfully, and wait mindfully. When leading others, it invites us to listen intently to what the other person is saying, hearing that person as if for the first time, being fully present to them (not being distracted by thoughts of the past or the future), letting their words soak in, and intuiting their emotions with gentleness and care.

We pay attention to what we are *sensitive* to. For example, some people are very sensitive to a crying baby in church. They might even turn and glare at the parents. Others might find it so normal that they barely notice. Still others might be so dialed into the liturgy that they pay very little attention to the crying.

We can practice selective attention by choosing our focus—and we can strengthen this ability with practice! We can choose to pay attention to the sense of hearing—or sight—or smell—or taste—or touch. That decision can change our perception of reality. What we are paying attention to in the words that another person is saying (what we are sensitive to) can change our perception of what that person is saying.

WITH PRACTICE, WE CAN STRENGTHEN OUR FOCUS AND ATTENTION.

To practice mindful leadership means to think about our thoughts, reflect on our feelings, and evaluate our behaviors. As we repeat the behaviors that are most healthy for our brains and eliminate those that are not, we change the neurological pathways in our brain. We reset the passwords in our brain. We change the way we interact with others. We become a better, more mindful, more heartful human being, more capable of leadership.

Mindful leadership means to suspend premature judgment of what the amygdala might perceive as an attack against us. Instead, we fire up the prefrontal cortex with heartfelt thoughts that consider the point of view of the other person.

Let's say you are in a parish council meeting and you are watching the meeting degrade into one boring report after another. Instead of focusing on what is going wrong, you can recalibrate your brain to focus on something more positive, perhaps what you are going to do next. Spend your mental energy on positive solutions instead of ruminating about negative behavior or obsessing over the problem. It is within your power to develop a positive mindset. Ask, What would it take to get this meeting back on track?

After the meeting, pray and reflect on the interaction. Talk to the people running the meeting and make positive suggestions for change. Come to the next meeting ready to share ideas about how your meetings can be more productive.

When you are in a meeting, mindfulness cultivates an awareness of your thoughts, emotions, and sensations. Your mind interprets what the brain is sensing. You can interrupt the negative self-talk in your brain. You can take a new view at what is being said and done. You can approach the here and now with greater curiosity. You can develop new habits of being open to other viewpoints. You can engage the heart and become kinder, more forgiving, and more focused on the positive and the beautiful, with intent and purpose.

THE MIND CAN IGNITE THE HEART.

The amygdala tends toward the negative. If we take the time to engage the left side of our prefrontal cortex, we can refocus on the positive. Focus on serving others. Connect to our higher purpose. Make an impact to improve the lives of others. Trust our conscience for guidance. This is mindful leadership.

Stewardship of Our Emotions

Employers are growing frustrated with what they say is a dearth of applicants who possess people skills. More than ever, employers are seeking candidates with people skills. A well-rounded candidate can work well with others, put their problem-solving skills to use in challenging situations, and be personable. Many employers complain that such employees are few and far between.

Emotional intelligence has been described by Daniel Goleman and subsequent research as a more accurate predictor of leadership success than technical or cognitive skills. In fact, your *emotional quotient* (EQ) is a better predictor of success in life and leadership than is your intelligence quotient (IQ).

A high EQ unleashes your full IQ potential. A low EQ limits your potential because fear, anger, worry, prejudice, jealousy, anxiety, and ignorance will limit your performance. The IQ is described by Goleman as a "threshold competence." It gets you in the door for an interview, and possibly gets you hired. But EQ is a "distinguishing competence" that will set you apart as a top performer after you are hired (Goleman).

EQ IS A BETTER PREDICTOR OF LEADERSHIP SUCCESS THAN IQ.

This is my take on the four areas that add up to emotional intelligence:

1. Self-Awareness (Mindfulness) = ability to be aware of your own emotions

2. Self-Control = ability to guide your own behaviors

3. Social Awareness (Empathy) = ability to identify with the emotions of others

4. Social Skills = ability to handle the emotions for others

	Awareness	Skills
Self	Mindfulness	Self-Control
Social	Empathy	Social Skills

Four Aspects of Emotional Intelligence

Note: I would suggest that we should add what would be a fifth dimension of emotional intelligence: Awareness of God and how God moves in our lives. While I have seen nothing written about this, I believe that prayerfulness is the real secret to awareness in self and others. To become truly awake to the way the Holy Spirit moves and breathes and dwells in our midst—this fosters the same type of self-reflection that we need to become more emotionally intelligent.

Self-Awareness (Mindfulness)

Self-awareness begins when we pause long enough to be awake to our emotions and aware of how they are impacting our thoughts, intentions, and behaviors. As human beings, we have this incredible ability to think about our thoughts, reflect on our emotions, consider our intentions, and evaluate our behaviors. Psalm 119 is a reflection on how happiness comes to those who ponder their ways, seek God with their whole heart, and fix their eyes on his ways.

Self-awareness happens in what Victor Frankl describes as that magical moment "between stimulus and response." It is that moment between sensation and action, between the trigger event and your reaction to it. It is in that moment of reflection, when we stop long enough to open our mind, our heart, and our will—so we can think, feel, and choose differently.

That slight pause is a *moment of grace*, a moment in time that presents itself only when we become fully awake to the present moment. Self-awareness helps us sense a change in emotions and understand what that change is doing to our physical energy and how it is affecting our thoughts and actions.

EMOTIONAL INTELLIGENCE BEGINS WITH SELF-AWARENESS.

Let's say you are still sitting in that boring parish council meeting. The moment you identify your emotion as *boredom*, you become self-aware. Boredom can have an impact on your thoughts, emotions, intentions, and behaviors. Perhaps your thoughts have strayed from the content of the meeting. Perhaps you are looking at your phone. Others might notice you are bored before you do. When you project boredom, you send a message to the person speaking that you are no longer interested in them or what they are saying.

Most of the time, we are oblivious to the impact that our emotions are having on our behavior—and that of others! Changing our behavior in that meeting begins with self-awareness. Especially when we are practicing leadership, our emotional reactions can be under a microscope. The emotions of the rest of the team can be dependent on the emotions of the leader. They are looking for cues as to how they should react.

THE LEADER'S EMOTIONS ARE CONTAGIOUS.

Somewhere between the moment of a stimulus and the moment of our response is an *opportunity for leadership*. In that moment of grace, we can be mindful. We can think about our thoughts, our plans, our intentions, and our reactions in real time. We can engage the heart by empathizing about what others are going through.

Research by Daniel Goleman shows that without self-awareness, it is very unlikely that we will practice any of the other three areas of emotional intelligence: self-control, social awareness, or social skills.

Self-Control

If self-awareness presents us with the dashboard of our emotions, *self-control* is the ability to use that information to guide our own behavior. When we become aware, we can begin to practice self-control. However, sometimes we just don't care enough or we don't want to change our behavior. Perhaps we think we can get what we want by acting angry, bored, frustrated, or upset.

Let's say you are running that parish council meeting. You might be able to get upset and bully people to get what you want—temporarily. But the results will be fleeting. People living in a dictatorship will comply only if they have no other choice. In a voluntary organization, like a church, people can choose to quit, leave for another church, or stop attending church altogether. The ones who stay will give you *compliance* but no more than that. You will have to try something else to get *above-and-beyond* behavior from your people.

Anger blinds us to the perspective of others. The signal for anger immediately sends adrenaline to our fists. This probably explains why we want to hit something when we get angry. Anger without self-awareness can be disastrous for our meetings.

SELF-CONTROL REQUIRES SELF-AWARENESS.

On the other hand, the signal for fear sends adrenaline to our feet. It makes us want to run away. When the leader of a group explodes with anger, some people in the room are likely to become afraid. They will want to run.

Anger can damage our ability to feel empathy. Fear can impair our ability to take risks, even prudent ones. Worry can drain us of the energy we need for leadership. Negative emotions that are not managed well can destroy us—and those around us.

Emotionally intelligent leaders use their self-awareness to reflect on how to change their interactions with others. They gain a more objective view of reality. They reshape their behaviors. They choose to go a different route.

Acting without self-awareness is like driving a car without a gauge that measures your engine temperature. Self-awareness without self-control is like continuing to drive your car even after you become aware that the gauge shows that the engine has boiled over.

Reflection on our behavior can break the vicious cycle of emotional outbursts and mindful regrets. Reflection occurs in the prefrontal cortex (PFC). It allows for a more refined, balanced, and mindful approach. The PFC can serve as the place where a reappraisal of the situation can take place. It is the place where mindful planning and organizing of ideas can occur—if we can guide our thoughts through reflection.

Self-monitoring is the ability to reflect on your cycle of behavior on a regular basis. Ask yourself, How aware was I of the emotions I experienced in that last meeting? How well did I manage those emotions? What could I do differently the next time John acts like that in a meeting?

PRAYERFUL PEOPLE FIND TIME FOR SELF-REFLECTION.

In a community like a parish, with all its intricate relationships, we need to find time in our daily lives to *reflect* on our behavior. We also need trusted people around us who will give us both positive and critical feedback.

Collectively, we also need to reflect on our interaction. Parish meetings should conclude with a moment of evaluation. One way to do this is to simply ask people to describe their thoughts or feelings about the meeting, in a simple word or a phrase, before adjournment. With more time, you can also ask people to conduct a *Plus Delta* evaluation, where they express what went well (the Plus) and what could change for the better (the Delta).

Yes, we have the ability as human beings to think about our thoughts and reflect on our actions. But if we want to go deeper, if we want to express our emotions in a healthy way, we need to create enough time to reflect in this busy world full of distractions.

Social Awareness (Empathy)

Social awareness is the ability to be aware of the emotions of others. It allows us to see how our interactions are affecting the emotions in the room. This requires great empathy, which can be very difficult to attain when you are experiencing emotional trauma yourself.

SOCIAL AWARENESS IS THE EMOTIONAL LITERACY

TO READ FACES, GESTURES, AND WORDS.

Let's say you are in a meeting. It is getting very heated. Your own emotions are sending adrenaline through your veins. Empathy is the ability to get outside of your own emotional reactions, to think outside your selfish ego and to relate to others. It is the ability to think with your heart and identify with the emotional reactions of others in the room.

Empathy is a choice. When the amygdala is screaming for attention, trying to tell you, "*So and so is attacking you,*" or "*You don't have to take that kind of treatment from anyone,*" empathy can enter in—if you engage the heart. Empathy calls you to pay attention to the needs and interests of others. When you are upset yourself, empathy is very counterintuitive.

Sympathy is more of an instinctive response. It means to "feel sorry" for someone. You hear about someone who just lost a spouse, or you see a homeless mother and child on the street, and you automatically feel sympathy. That is not empathy.

The plasticity of the brain allows for retraining to become more empathetic, more positive and more aware of what is going on around us. We can train ourselves to become more empathetic by developing stronger connections between the brain and the heart. Interestingly, research shows that we can strengthen the neural connection between head and heart through religious practices such as reading Scripture, attending Mass, singing hymns and chants, saying the rosary, or engaging in eucharistic adoration (Begley).

To be empathetic is to choose the heart over the amygdala. Empathy is a leap of faith. It requires mindful attention to listen to the heart center, which is signaling us to consider someone else. When we can turn off the loud voice of the amygdala, and involve our heart in decision-making, we choose faith over fear, wisdom over control, humility over pride, and altruism over selfishness.

Social Skills

Imagine you are in that parish council meeting. Things are getting emotional. To facilitate the inter-action of your team during these moments, you need to try: (1) to be attentive to your own emotions, (2) to guide your behaviors despite your own emotions, (3) to pick up on the emotions of others, and (4) to act with empathy toward others in the room.

Our ability to empathize is strongly related to our emotional security. When we are enduring an amyg-dala hijack, it becomes very difficult to think about others. We may need to calm our rage, control our fear, or console our frustrations before we can think straight.

Emotions are contagious. Seeing a person cry can bring on your own tears. Hearing others laugh can make you laugh until you cry. The emotions of a leader have a special effect on the whole team. The more the leader can create an atmosphere of emotional security, the more people will act with empathy.

EMPATHY CAN BE CONTAGIOUS.

The first step in guiding the interaction of a team during an emotional episode is to demonstrate empathy. When a leader shows empathy, it has a multiplying effect on the rest of the community. The people are more likely to empathize as well, to trust each other, to collaborate with each other, to work as a team, to help each other out, to take the initiative on new projects, to participate in the activities of the parish, and to develop themselves as disciples.

Dr. Kent Brantley, who contracted Ebola while practicing medicine in Liberia, upon his return, said on National Public Radio, "We cannot let our sense of fear trump our sense of compassion." Basically, he was asking the Good Samaritan question, *"If I do not stop to help these people with Ebola, what will happen to them?"*

Acting with empathy changes the wiring inside our very own brains. When we care for each other as a community, nurture each other through the rough times, and improve the interaction of the congre-gation, we not only change the connections in our community, we *change the neural connections in our own brains*. We strengthen the neurological trail between the head and the heart—the path to empathy.

Forgiving someone else of their transgressions against us is an empathetic action that can occur through prayer, reflection, and the sacrament of reconciliation. The amygdala will tell us to exchange an "eye for an eye." It will seek revenge. It will harbor resentment. Yet revenge and resentment are not healthy for our hearts, our minds, our bodies—or our relationships. Reconciliation is the healthier response.

Jesus says, "You shall love your neighbor *as yourself*" (emphasis mine) (Matt 22:39). Love of neigh-bor involves love of self. Empathy takes us in the healthy direction of loving self. For example, when we forgive others, we can be expressing love for our self.

"Forgive us our debts, *as we also have forgiven our debtors*" (emphasis mine) (Matt 6:12). God for-gives us. We forgive others. In the process, we forgive ourselves. It is in our best interest to let go of the anger, jealousy, or resentment.

We live with many regrets for *yesterday* and worries about *tomorrow*. Neither of these will help us live in the *present* moment—to be present to the present. In fact, the two biggest obstacles to living fully in the present moment are (1) the past and (2) the future.

To act with all four steps of emotional intelligence, we must be fully awake to the present moment. We cannot be distracted by regrets from the past or worries about the future.

Chapter Summary

In this chapter, we explored how improving the stewardship of our own hearts and minds is essential training for leadership. Whether you are pastoring a church, such as Fr. Dave, or you are a layperson preparing to lead change, the first step is your own formation. Forming hearts and minds helps us become human beings fully capable of leading change.

The next chapter looks at how to engage the hearts and minds of members of the parish so that they are contributing the best of their gifts and talents. Leadership enables others to become the best version of themselves. Fr. Dave's pastoral approach can encourage or discourage lay leadership and lay engagement.

References

Begley, Sharon. *Train Your Mind, Change Your Brain: How a New Science Reveals Our Extraordinary Potential to Transform Ourselves*. New York: Ballantine Books, 2007.

Bourgeault, Cynthia. *The Wisdom Jesus: Transforming Heart and Mind—a New Perspective on Christ and His Message*. Boston, MA: Shambhala Publications, 2008.

Bradberry, Travis, and Jean Greaves. *Emotional Intelligence 2.0*. San Diego, CA: TalentSmart, 2009.

Davidson, Richard J., and Sharon Begley. *The Emotional Life of Your Brain*. New York: Hudson Street Press, 2012.

Dimitriadis, Nikolaos, and Alexandros Psychogios. *Neuroscience for Leaders: A Brain-Adaptive Approach*. London: Kogan Page Unlimited, 2016.

Goleman, Daniel. *Emotional Intelligence*. New York: Bantam Dell, 2005.

Heifetz, Ronald A., and Marty Linsky. *Leadership on the Line: Staying Alive through the Dangers of Leading*. Boston: Harvard Business School Press, 2002.

King, Martin Luther, Jr. "I've Been to the Mountaintop" speech, April 3, 1968.

Kouzes, James M., and Barry Z. Posner. *The Truth about Leadership: The No-Fads, Heart-of-the-Matter, Things You Need to Know*. San Francisco: Jossey-Bass, 2010.

Newburg, Andrew, and Mark Robert Waldman. *Words Can Change Your Brain: 12 Conversation Strategies to Build Trust, Resolve Conflict, and Increase Intimacy*. New York: Hudson Street Press, 2012.

Nouwen, Henri. *In the Name of Jesus: Reflections on Christian Leadership*. New York: The Crossroads Publishing Company, 1989.

Oswald, Roy M., and Arland Jacobsen. *The Emotional Intelligence of Jesus: Relational Smarts for Religious Leaders*. Lanham, MD: The Rowman & Littlefield Publishing Group, 2015.

Pope St. John Paul II. *Centesimus Annus*. Rome: Libreria Editrice Vaticana, 1991.

Rost, Joseph C. *Leadership for the Twenty-First Century*. New York: Praeger Publishers, 1991.

Scharmer, Otto, and Katrin Kaufer. *Leading from the Emerging Future: From Ego-System to Eco-System Economies: Applying Theory U to Transforming Business, Society and Self*. San Francisco: Berrett-Koehler Publishers, 2013.

Schein, Edgar H. *Humble Inquiry: The Gentle Art of Asking Instead of Telling*. San Francisco: Berrett-Koehler Publishers, 2013.

Senge, Peter M., C. Otto Scharmer, Joseph Jaworski, and Betty Sue Flowers. *Presence: Human Purpose and the Field of the Future*. New York: Crown Publishing House, 2004.

Chapter 2

Engaging Parishioners

Chapter 2 Preview

In this chapter, we explore the following:

- How Fr. Dave's actions can encourage or discourage leadership
- How a culture of *engagement* can enhance all areas of ministry
- The role of the pastor in a *consultative hierarchy*
- *Servant leadership* and how it fits parish life
- The upside and downside of *charismatic leadership*
- How leaders can be assertive and cooperative at the same time

St. Michael's Parish—Encouraging Parishioner Engagement and Initiative

Fr. Dave was preparing for Mass when he noticed Sam O'Donnell arriving about fifteen minutes early. Sam walked to the front door of the church but spotted something wrong. He turned around and headed back toward his pickup truck. He grabbed his tool box, and within a few minutes, he fixed the front door of the church, which had not been swinging properly for quite some time. Sam proceeded to make it into his pew before Mass began.

After Mass, Sam stuck around for the monthly potluck held at the church. He laughed as he added his store-bought cookies to the tables full of homemade foods. He didn't have time to bake anything that weekend because he had been busy with spring planting on his family farm. Sam began making the rounds visiting with his fellow parishioners when Fr. Dave walked over.

How Fr. Dave responds at this point can make all the difference. It will determine whether laypeople will be reluctant or encouraged to take initiative and practice leadership.

What Is Engagement?

Research shows that about two of every three people are not *engaged* in their workplace (Thomas). They are just going through the motions. Maybe they have "golden handcuffs," which means that the money they receive at work is too much to give up for another job. They work just enough so they are not fired but nothing above and beyond that.

ENGAGEMENT COMES FROM THE HEART.

Engagement has become a watch word for many businesses. Same for parishes. When I conduct strategic planning for parishes, the top challenges identified tend to include lay engagement, increased participation, or more involvement.

What do we mean by *engagement*? In the workplace, *engagement* means that the employees are "actively self-managing their work," according to Kenneth Thomas. It means that the people have *bought in* to the point where they need little or no management from the outside. Like Sam, they take the initiative when they see something that needs to be done.

Engagement cannot be coerced. It is a *voluntary* activity. It comes from the heart.

If you want engagement, try *intrinsic motivators*. If you want the people to self-manage, those in positions of authority must resist the temptation to overmanage or micromanage. Command and control tactics discourage self-management. They deter engagement.

Lay engagement means that the parishioners are intrinsically motivated to fully participate in the life of the parish.

According to Thomas, there are four sources of intrinsic motivation:

1. Meaningfulness—connecting all ministry to a sense of purpose and direction

2. Choice—giving people some options on how to get involved in ministry

3. Competence—developing the gifts and talents (*charisms*) of the laity

4. Progress—demonstrating how their efforts are making a difference in accomplishing the purpose (*mission*) and reaching the direction (*vision*) of the parish.

A Culture of Engagement

In some churches, the pastor might not take too kindly to someone showing up for Mass and taking out their tools to fix the front door. Especially in a larger parish, it might be viewed as stepping on the toes of the maintenance staff. An order to fix the door might have to go through the buildings and grounds committee. It is up to leadership to establish an organizational culture that allows parishioners to take the initiative. When people see something that needs to be done (within reason), they do it.

This means a more engaged parish where people feel at home. Sam took care of the front door in the same way he would care for his farmhouse. All of this could change if Fr. Dave took the approach that everything needed to go through him first. For some pastors, the need for control can trump everything else.

Sam's action to fix the front door showed that he was *engaged* as a parishioner. He was self-motivated. He felt close to his fellow parishioners and treated them like family. In fact, Sam was so connected to the parish that he was considering enrollment in the diocesan pastoral ministry program, a lay formation training for those who want to get more involved.

SERVANT LEADERSHIP INSPIRES ORGANIZATIONAL CITIZENSHIP.

His level of engagement is a testament to Fr. Dave, to the other parish staff, and to the leadership of the parish. He demonstrated what sociologists call *organizational citizenship behaviors*—such as helping, participating, initiating, and self-developing. We might call them *discipleship behaviors*. An overwhelming volume of research shows that organizational citizenship behaviors are a sign of effective leadership, such as servant leadership (Organ, Podsakoff, and MacKenzie).

Servant leadership is leading like Jesus. Leaders are "not to be served but to serve" (Matt 20:28; Mark 10:45). Servant leadership is following the example of Jesus when he washed the feet of his disciples (John 13:1–17). Servant leaders place themselves at the service of the people, the mission, and the vision.

When leaders invite, inspire, and influence the members with servant leadership behaviors, the people respond with *discipleship behaviors*. Imagine if the pastor or someone in authority had scolded Sam for fixing the door. That would be demotivating. It would stifle engagement. On the other hand, servant leadership inspires engagement.

The Church is a *voluntary* organization. According to the *Catechism of the Catholic Church* and the Third Commandment, Sunday Mass attendance is an obligation. However, the reality is that people *voluntarily* join, attend, contribute, and participate in a church. That is why *engagement* is such a watchword in today's Church. Voluntary participation cannot be coerced.

Interestingly, we also define *leadership* as a voluntary activity.

Bosses gain compliance. Leaders get engagement. Leaders engage people in noncoercive forms of influence. When you engage people, you get more *intrinsic* motivation. When you coerce people, you are not engaging or leading.

Leadership is neither pushing nor pulling. It grants *free will* to the followers. To reach engagement, you touch hearts and minds—and eventually their wills.

A Consultative Hierarchy

Yes, the Church is hierarchical. It fits what John Rawls calls a *consultative hierarchy*, where those in charge make decisions based on the common good of all. Canon law requires that the pastor has the final say in all matters of the parish, but only after *consultation*.

As pastor, Fr. Dave has ultimate responsibility. His role is to insure the *Catholicity* of every decision that is made. This does not mean that every decision is to be made according to the whims of the pastor. The ultimate authority of the pastor is more akin to a supreme court decision than a presidential veto. The pastor makes sure that what the parish is deciding is a good fit for a Catholic church.

Let's say that the parish council wants to hold its annual dinner during the middle of Holy Week. Fr. Dave knows this is not good timing. Not for him. Nor for the parish community. He could just veto the decision. However, it might be wiser to listen patiently to the people and then to explain to them *why* this is not a good idea. It is better to persuade than to dictate.

With a reasonable explanation, Fr. Dave could convince people that holding an annual dinner during Holy Week would not be in the best interests of St. Michael's Parish. This is the most important week of the year liturgically. All emphasis needs to be there. However, dictating any decision, especially without explanation, will dampen the enthusiasm of some parishioners. Explaining *why* turns the discussion into a teachable moment.

It is not only the content of *what* a parish decides that is important, but also *how* that decision is made. Americans like to think that every institution should be a democracy. In such a culture, to lead with authority takes patience. Americans expect to be involved in the decision-making process. Only on rare occasions, that is, when the laity wants to make a change that clearly is *not Catholic*, or not in the common good of the Catholic community, should a pastor make an executive decision, and even then, only with dialogue and explanation.

Discussion Question

Under what circumstances should a pastor veto the decision of a parish council?

Bishop Thomas Zinkula was participating in a dialogue with newly ordained priests when this topic emerged. His insight: If the parish council is considering something that might not be Catholic, or if the pastor thinks the idea is not in the best interests of the community, or if the project is not within their capacity to accomplish, the pastor should let the council know his concerns *during* the conversation— not wait to veto afterward. In this way, the pastor would never have to veto a decision of the council—just raise concerns as they come up.

A *consultative hierarchy* means genuine consultation and honest dialogue, back and forth. True dialogue creates a culture that allows for lay leadership to emerge. Parish leadership can occur when any parishioner increases the motivation, inspires the confidence, and raises the competence of others to join in a change effort. This leads to a greater sense of engagement.

As leaders of a voluntary organization, parish leaders must find voluntary ways of motivating, that is, *intrinsic motivators*. The use of coercive tactics, even in a church with the hierarchical structure of the Catholic Church, lowers the engagement of the people.

PARISH LEADERSHIP IS DONE THROUGH, WITH, AND BY A COMMUNITY.

To get engagement, you need to get buy-in. Like any other matter of the heart, buy-in cannot be dictated, but it can be encouraged. Ironically, when people are fully engaged, they will need less over-sight. Authority and control are less needed when the people are engaged. They can self-manage when engaged.

Leading Stewardship and Evangelization

Let's say your parish council has decided that its top two priorities are to become: (1) more inviting (*evangelization*) and (2) more welcoming (*stewardship*).

Evangelization and stewardship are critically important to the American Church. It is interesting to contrast the situation in the United States with that of Europe. Churches in Europe rely more on funds from foundations and governments—and much less from Sunday collections. These foundations and governmental sources of funding require lots of data.

The result is that European churches tend to appeal to the *cognitive* function of the brain. On the other hand, American churches do better to appeal to the *heart*. In the United States, nonprofits (including churches) raise about 72 percent of all income from individuals. The number is even higher for churches.

EVANGELIZATION TOUCHES THE HEART.
STEWARDSHIP GIVES FROM THE HEART.

People in the United States are less motivated by data that appeal to the head and more motivated by stories that appeal to the heart. As a result, it makes sense that in the United States, we emphasize both evangelization (*speaking to the heart*) and stewardship (*giving from the heart*).

St. Paul tells us that "God loves a cheerful giver" (2 Cor 9:7). A cheerful giver has a big heart. The steward gives without asking whether the receiver has merit. Instead of giving to a need, the steward gives out of a *need to give*, not looking for anything in return. That need to give comes from a grateful heart.

Research at Notre Dame suggests that people are more generous when supporting a *mission* than when giving to a specific *need* (Starks and Smith). If you fundraise for a roof, people will give until the roof is repaired. If you fundraise for a mission, people will continue to give to that mission.

STEWARDSHIP IS A VOLUNTARY CHOICE.

To lead a ministry of stewardship requires countercultural measures. Many Catholics consider *stewardship* a Protestant word. Many think it is just about money. Parish leaders might begin with a study of the 1992 pastoral letter *Stewardship: A Disciple's Response*. This letter articulates the core of the stewardship message:

- Discipleship is a conscious choice to follow Jesus.
- Stewardship is a response to the call to be a disciple.
- Stewardship is a life-changing experience of conversion.
- All of this involves *"life-shaping changes of mind and heart."*

The pastoral letter defines a *steward* as someone who "receives God's gifts gratefully, cherishes and tends to them in a responsible and accountable manner, shares them in justice and love with others, and returns them with increase to the Lord." That says it all.

Note: There is nothing about stewardship that can be coerced. Stewardship is a voluntary commitment. It comes *from the heart*. In this sense, the heart is not a physical pump or an emotional center. It is the center of our spiritual perception. It is the source of wisdom.

Jesus demonstrates the challenges of evangelization in the story of Luke 5:1–11. His disciples had been fishing all night without catching any fish. He invites them to cast their nets back into deep waters. They probably looked at him like he was crazy. It's not like they had not tried both sides of the boat. They could have said, "We tried that before and it didn't work." But when they catch boatloads of fish, they become astonished. Jesus' response is to encourage their hearts: "Do not be afraid" (Luke 5:10).

EVANGELIZATION IS SPEAKING FROM HEART TO HEART.

To lead a ministry of evangelization, you need to encourage the hearts of people, so they are willing to try something new, or to try something old in a new way. Evangelization is taking the risk of talking about your faith. It is talking about your faith with a little more heart—without being afraid. Like Jesus, we need to invite others to "come and see" (John 1:39). We also need to "go...and make disciples" (Matt 28:19).

Evangelization requires hearts filled with more hope and less fear. Jesus fills his disciples with hope when he says, "Look around you, and see how the fields are ripe for harvesting" (John 4:35). In another passage, Jesus adds, "but the laborers are few" (Luke 10:2).

To lead evangelization ministry is to create a *culture* where people are willing to share their faith passionately with others. In a parish, this begins with opportunities for parishioners to "encounter Christ in a life-changing way in the context of a parish," as Sherry Weddell puts it. Evangelization will not happen unless and until we have encountered Christ personally.

When Mark says that Jesus' "fame began to spread" (Mark 1:28), what did that look like? People were walking for miles to hear Jesus. They were talking up their faith through all of Galilee. This was *the first evangelization*: followers who were fueled with a passion became evangelists.

Interestingly, all this happened without the help of social media or television. It happened when people talked to each other, face to face, heart to heart. It happened because their *hearts were on fire*. That is essential for evangelization.

As Catholics, we tend to think negatively about the word *evangelical*. To change our way of thinking about evangelization is part of the cultural change needed in the Church. It will take *countercultural* measures to get Catholics to open up and share their faith. Leading cultural change begins by changing one behavior at a time.

You cannot force people to become stewards or evangelists. You cannot "guilt" them into it. Leading change in stewardship and evangelization calls for different forms of influence. It takes leadership that *stirs the heart*. One way is through servant leadership.

Servant Leadership

Servant leadership is a term coined by Robert Greenleaf, who said that servant leadership starts with the motivation "first to serve and then to lead." In the process of serving, a person sees something they want to change. They begin to influence others to join them in making that change, and...they are leading. In fact, they are *servant leading*.

But it doesn't stop there, because it is so easy to slip into narcissism when called upon to lead. To practice servant leadership means to constantly reflect on how and what you are doing, and why you are doing it. Is it about others? Or has it become all about me? Servant leadership is an iterative process of prayer, reflection, and action. It requires mindfulness. This includes a continuous *examination of conscience*.

SERVANT LEADERSHIP IS NOT JUST A BOSS WHO HAPPENS TO BE A NICE GUY.

Servant leadership can include simple acts of kindness, watching to see what others need and taking care to meet those needs. It is more than just being a "nice boss" because (1) servant leadership is not a position and (2) it requires that you are changing something. If you are not changing something, you are not leading. If you are not leading, you are not servant leading. Servant leaders change things.

Servant leaders use power as a means to an end, not as an end unto itself.

The major difference between servant leadership and other forms of leadership is the motivation of the leader. In servant leadership, the *motivation to serve* stems from a heart that is committed to something larger than yourself: (1) devotion to a mission, (2) service to the people being led, and (3) a faith commitment to God.

Service adds to the authenticity and builds the credibility of the leader. Management guru Peter Drucker once said that the key to business is to *serve your people and they will serve your customer*. For parishes, we could say, *Love your people and they will love you back*.

Pope Francis distinguishes between *servanthood*, where someone is treated as a servant and their dignity is diminished, and *service*, where a person chooses to serve someone out of love and respect. The difference is choice. Servant leadership does not coerce. It allows the other person to choose to follow.

To lead and to follow is a choice. It is a calling. When we servant lead, or choose to follow a servant leader, we are choosing to be of service to God, to others, and to a mission. Service is another factor that cannot be coerced. It comes from the heart.

Research shows that servant leadership can enhance intrinsic motivation (Ebener). It instills trust and confidence in the people being servant led. It inspires the people to participate, to take initiative, to help each other, and to develop themselves as disciples of Jesus. It inspires people to go above and beyond.

Parish Activity

Ask each member of your group to write down the name of a great leader.
Ask: Who comes to mind when you think of the greatest leaders?
Discuss: Was this person someone you know? Is this person still alive?
Why is it that so many of us think of famous dead people when identifying great leaders?
What can we do to change that?

Kenotic Leadership

Servant leadership could also be described as *kenotic leadership*.

The Greek word *kenosis* means "to empty" or "to let go," as in Philippians 2:7, where Paul says that Jesus "emptied himself" to be born "in human likeness." In 1 Corinthians 2:16, Paul teaches us to put on the "mind of Christ," which means to *empty* our selfish concerns and instead, to align our mind, our heart, and our spirit with that of Christ. Kenosis aligns our mind with the mind of Christ.

Kenosis is abundant love beyond reason, love beyond the human capacity to understand it. It is heavenly love, not earthly love. This love is the vision that Jesus speaks of as the kingdom of God. It is love given for the pure sake of love. It is a love that rings true of the love among Father, Son, and Holy Spirit. It is emptying the self for the sake of the other.

KENOTIC LEADERSHIP TAKES ON THE MIND OF CHRIST.

A kenotic leader would be emptied of the temptations for power and prestige, emptied of the need for control, and totally devoted to the service of God and his people. The kenotic leader would look for the good in others, forgive others for their self-serving ways, and bring out the *best version of them-selves and others*. Kenosis is the opposite of command and control.

The kenotic path can be described as the distance between the heart and the brain. Communication along this path is strengthened with spiritual practices. Cynthia Bourgeault suggests this might explain why Mary Magdalen could communicate with Jesus in the garden of Gethsemane; why Jesus could forgive Peter for his denial; and why "their hearts were burning" when the disciples met Jesus on the path to Emmaus.

Charismatic Leadership

Some pastors bring great energy to a parish. They are outgoing and magnetic. The people are drawn to the pastor and the pastor is devoted to the people. An emotional bond is created that stirs great loyalty to that pastor.

This can be described as *charismatic leadership*. But not all charismatic people are leaders. Some are coercive, which disqualifies them for leadership. If the people are not participating voluntarily, it is not leadership.

Charisma has its advantages and disadvantages. The advantage is that it can create bursts of positive energy. The people are enthused about the parish. They are more engaged and more willing to go above and beyond.

Charisma in Greek means "gift from God." This explains why the Greeks thought that leaders were born, not made. They equated charisma with leadership and did not view charisma as something you developed.

Charisma can be a gift. It can be a gift to energize people in this way. There are skills associated with charisma that can also be learned. Charismatic people can motivate and mobilize people with speaking, writing, or preaching. They have excellent communication skills.

Having charisma does not automatically qualify you for leadership. But it is possible to lead with charisma—if you can resist the temptation toward narcissism.

Jesus had charisma. Consider how the "great crowds" gathered to hear Jesus (Matt 4:25). Martin Luther King Jr. inspired a civil rights movement with his sermons and speeches. Gandhi was able to bring a nation to its knees by fasting almost to his death. Charisma can move large numbers of people.

However, there is a downside to charisma. Think of the terrible despots who mobilized the masses to become blindly obedient. Obedience is a virtue but not when it is blind to the morals of the so-called leader.

CHARISMA DOES NOT ALWAYS MEAN LEADERSHIP.

Charismatic pastors can create an overly dependent, super-loyal, and unhealthy bond with their parishioners. In extreme cases, the people begin to worship the pastor. The charismatic pastor can be perceived by some as the embodiment of the Church itself.

Charismatic leadership is overrated. In many cases, it is not even leadership. Granted, it can generate lots of energy for the vision of the charismatic person, but it has serious downsides. Rare are the examples of charismatic people who are servant leaders. Charismatic people tend toward *narcissism*. As they become more and more popular, the praise and loyalty that mounts can be a huge obstacle to servant leadership. It takes great self-awareness to maintain humility in the face of such popularity.

Strength of character is more important than personal magnetism.

Q4 Leadership

Task and *relationship* are the yin and yang of leadership and management. In Chinese philosophy, the yin and yang describe a *dualism* that exists when seemingly opposite forces are complementary, interconnected, or perhaps even interdependent.

The yin and yang can give rise to each other. Natural dualities such as light and dark, male and female, fire and water are examples of the yin and yang. For instance, the shadow cannot exist without light. The male cannot exist without the female. Fire cannot exist without the water that feeds the wood that the fire will burn.

In the same way, it is hard to conceive of a relationship that is completely divorced from a task. Completing a task can forge a relationship. Building a relationship can hasten the completion of a task. The task and relationship are reciprocal forces that complement each other in a way that forms a whole that is greater than its parts.

Let's say you are trying to build the team spirit in your parish council. If you can get the parish council to work as a team, you will be more likely to succeed in whatever task the council takes up. Similarly, as the parish council becomes more and more successful in accomplishing its tasks, the relationships will grow more loyal, trusting, and committed to each other.

Using the task and the relationship as the two major components of leadership, we can draw the model of leadership behavior seen in the figure below (Lefton and Buzzotta). Here, we measure *assertiveness* on the task vertically and the *warmth* of the relationship horizontally.

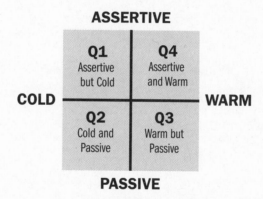

Q1 behavior is cold and dominant. It has little or no regard for others. This behavior is prevalent among people who have authority, especially those who lack confidence. The greater the authority, the more we tend to act in Q1. Somehow, having formal power tempts us to impose our will on others, without consideration of the views of others. Q1 is easier than the collaborative work of Q4 leadership.

Q4 IS THE OPTIMAL APPROACH.

Q2 behavior is cold and passive. It is common to see Q2 behavior when a person has been under the grip of prolonged Q1 behavior. When a person gets beat up time and again with Q1 behavior, they can feel defeated. They can regress into Q2 passivity. Q1 behavior may get short-term results, especially in emergency situations, or when the people have no alternative except to comply. However, in a voluntary situation like a parish, people will eventually choose to leave the Q1 authority figure. In the interim, they act with Q2 behavior.

Q3 is warm on the relationship but soft on the task. It is common to see Q3 behavior in social organizations like nonprofits, schools, hospitals, and churches. A pastor friend of mine readily admits his tendency to be a *people pleaser*. When you worry too much about whether other people like you, you tend to act with Q3 behavior. If you are a people pleaser, it might help to remind yourself that if the people are committed to the mission (the task), they will be more "pleased" when they see progress toward the mission.

Q4 is the best approach. It is highest in concern for the task and the relationship. It is assertive on the task and warm on the relationship—at the same time! Whether we are leaders or followers, administrators or ministers, managers or direct reports, the optimal behavior is Q4. To act with Q4 is be passionate about the mission and vision while also collaborative, considerate, and supportive of others as we pursue that mission.

Another way to think of Q4 is *"speaking the truth in love"* (Eph 4:15). To speak the truth is to be assertive—without being aggressive or passive. Doing so in love is to act with the mind and heart of Christ (1 Cor 2:16).

Reflection Questions

The optimal approach to leadership is to practice Q4 behavior.

- When you move out of Q4, what direction do you usually move: Q1, Q2, or Q3?
- Under what circumstances are you inclined to move toward Q1, Q2, or Q3?

Team Leadership

A familiar adage in community organizing is this: "If you want to go fast, go alone. If you want to go far, go with a team." Leadership is a collective activity that involves a team.

The best ideas usually emerge from a team when they reach some sort of *synergy*. Synergy happens when the combined energy of a team achieves a result better than any one of us could have come up with on our own. My idea bounces off your idea and we come up with a new, collaborative idea.

LEADERSHIP IS AN INTERACTIVE RELATIONSHIP.

The best ideas in parish planning tend to emerge out of the synergy that results from real dialogue. At my parish in Iowa, some people on the hospitality team wanted to connect members of the parish to each other. As Michael Havercamp tells it, they saw evangelization as "the essential mission of the Church" and recognized "that evangelization happens through relationships."

They entered into dialogue about the mission of the parish and the ministry of the hospitality team. They figured that if we are supposed to be the people of God when we worship together, we need to know each other. What emerged out of the conversation was the launch of a program called "Guess Who Is Coming to Dinner?" One family agrees to host dinner and the parish picks people to be on the invited list. The hosts of the program do not know who is coming to dinner until the guests arrive at the door. The goal is simply to build relationships.

Relationships change everything. Being in relationship with someone else can change your perspective about that person. Once you begin to empathize with another person's situation, you are less inclined to judge that person and more likely to be open to their ideas. That is why it is so important on parish councils and commissions that the planners get to know each other personally. It builds trust, commitment, and cohesion, which is *social capital*.

Followership

Geese fly in a "V" formation to create synergy. By going ahead of the group, the lead goose creates uplift. This reduces the air friction for the rest of the flock. A team of geese can accomplish much more than any one single goose. The role of being the lead goose takes extra energy. Therefore, the geese rotate between leadership and followership. When the lead goose gets tired, it steps back and allows another goose to take the lead.

Parish Activity

Let's say you are chair of a parish council or commission and you want to encourage everyone to get to know each other better. One way to do this is to take several minutes at the beginning of your meetings to allow people to spend about five to ten minutes visiting with each other. Allow them to introduce themselves (if necessary), and then to visit, personally, one-on-one, with someone else in the room.

As they get to know each other, give them a question to discuss, such as the following:

- What motivated you to join this commission?
- What can we do to grow this area of ministry (name an area)?
- How have you encountered Christ in your life?
- How do you think the work of this commission fits the mission of the parish, that is, to enable people to encounter Christ in their lives?

My parish suggests that at each meeting, one person responds to this last question and shares their faith story with the whole group. This can be a powerful experience that builds relationships and prepares people to feel more comfortable evangelizing about their faith.

The geese exhibit what followership is all about. Some view the word *follower* as negative. Others, such as Joseph Rost, suggest that *followers* are those in training to become *leaders*. Followers and leaders exchange positions on a regular basis. Like the geese, we do leadership together, not individually. Followership becomes active preparation for leadership.

Likewise, people should rotate in and out of leadership roles on parish councils and commissions. When the same people carry the load for too long, they wear themselves out. Like the geese, they should create a vacuum for other leaders to emerge. New leadership should emerge with each new idea, for each new initiative, or with the various aspects of a new project.

FOLLOWERSHIP IS THE BEST TRAINING FOR LEADERSHIP.

In this way, members of the councils and commissions are *doing leadership together*. Followers should see themselves as equal to the leader but choosing in this instance to follow rather than lead.

Their turn to lead will come at a different time or on a different project. The main thing is that each new leader is committed to the overall mission of the parish. Leadership is an opportunity for everyone to gain a sense of purpose beyond themselves.

Leaders and followers rotate based on the level of interest and competence needed for each project. Everyone needs to find ways of working within their gifts and talents. Programs like *Strengths Finders* and *Called and Gifted* can help parishioners identify these gifts and talents. People find the most energy for a project when they are working within their charisms.

On the other hand, it is also helpful to continually learn and update your skills. Working outside your strengths might allow you to grow and stretch yourself. If followership is practiced as described here, eventually everyone on a team will improve their skills.

Active followership becomes the best preparation for leadership.

Involvement in any ministry can provide the practice you need to develop your leadership potential. You learn to lead by first being an active follower. Followers need to be courageous, honest, and credible. They are willing to speak up, especially when they disagree. If you are on a parish council or commission and see something that is wrong but say nothing, you are not practicing followership. That is conflict avoidance.

Just like leaders, followers give credit where credit is due. They admit mistakes, rather than blaming others. Followers are insightful, candid, and willing to take risks. They keep leaders and colleagues honest and informed. In fact, the best followers have the same qualities as leaders. The qualities you develop as an active follower will serve you well when you step up to lead.

Leaders become followers—and followers become leaders.

Virtues of Leadership

Approaching leadership as described here will require the following:

- *Humility*—to admit that you do not have all the answers
- *Patience*—to accept that real change will come slowly
- *Mercy*—to forgive yourself and others for mistakes

When we pray the words, "Our Father," we portray ourselves as brothers and sisters, sons and daughters, of the same God. That makes us all equals in God's eyes, whether we are leaders or followers, clergy or lay, engaged or inactive members of the parish. This is what the word *dignity* signifies. We are dignified, or "worthy," because we are all created in God's image and likeness, part of the same human family.

POPE FRANCIS IS LOOKING FOR HUMILITY, PATIENCE, AND MERCY IN HIS BISHOPS.

To see the leadership potential in someone else is to recognize their human dignity.

Chapter Summary

In this chapter, we focused on the leadership approaches that are most likely to enhance the *engagement* of the laity in a parish. It is particularly important for those leading from a position of authority to model *servant leadership*. This pastoral approach can encourage laypeople to step up and lead.

The next chapter explores the *interactive people skills* that are necessary to lead in a parish. The servant leadership approach is to listen first, then to build consensus through dialogue.

References

Bourgeault, Cynthia. *The Meaning of Mary Magdalene: Discovering the Woman at the Heart of Christianity*. Boulder, CO: Shambhala Publications, 2010.

——. *The Wisdom Jesus: Transforming Heart and Mind—a New Perspective on Christ and His Message*. Boston, MA: Shambhala Publications, 2008.

Called and Gifted Discernment Program. St. Catherine Siena Institute. www.siena.org/called-gifted.

Drucker, Peter F. *Managing the Non-Profit Organization: Principles and Practices*. New York: CollinsBusiness, 1990.

Giving USA. *The Annual Report on Philanthropy for the Year 2016*. 2017. www.GivingUSA.org.

Goleman, Daniel. *Emotional Intelligence*. New York: Bantam Dell, 2005.

Greenleaf, Robert K. *The Servant Leader Within: The Transformative Path*. Edited by Hamilton Beazley, Julie Beggs, and Larry C. Spears. Mahwah, NJ: Paulist Press, 2003.

House, Robert. "A 1976 Theory of Charismatic Leadership." Working Paper Series 76–06. Paper presented in Carbondale, IL, October 26–28, 1976.

Keith, Kent M. *The Case for Servant Leadership*. Westfield, IN: The Greenleaf Center for Servant Leadership, 2008.

Kouzes, James M., and Barry Z. Posner. *The Leadership Challenge*. 3rd ed. San Francisco, CA: Jossey-Bass, 2002.

Larson, Erik. "Diversity + Inclusion = Better Decision-Making at Work." *Forbes*. September 12, 2017.

Lefton, Robert E., and Victor R. Buzzotta. *Leadership through People Skills*. New York: McGraw-Hill, 2004.

Starks, Brian, and Christian Smith. *Unleashing Catholic Generosity: Explaining the Catholic Giving Gap in the United States*. University of Notre Dame Institute of Church Life, 2013.

Organ, Dennis W., Philip M. Podsakoff, and Scott B. MacKenzie. *Organizational Citizenship Behavior: Its Nature, Antecedents, and Consequences*. Thousand Oaks, CA: Sage Publications, 2006.

Pope Francis. *The Joy of the Gospel* (*Evangelii Gaudium*). Rome: Libreria Editrice Vaticana, 2013.

Rath, Tom. *Strengths Finder 2.0*. New York: Gallup Press, 2007.

Rost, Joseph C. *Leadership for the Twenty-First Century*. New York: Praeger Publishers, 1991.

Second Vatican Council. Constitution on the Sacred Liturgy (*Sacrosanctum Concilium*). Rome: Libreria Editrice Vaticana, 1963.

——. Decree on the Apostolate of the Laity of Vatican II (*Apostolicam Actuositatem*). Rome: Libreria Editrice Vaticana, 1965.

Thomas, Kenneth W. *Intrinsic Motivation at Work: What Really Drives Employee Engagement*. San Francisco: Berrett-Koehler Publishers, 2009.

United States Conference of Catholic Bishops. *Called and Gifted: The American Catholic Laity*. Washington, DC: Committee on the Laity, 1980.

———. *Stewardship: A Disciple's Response*. Washington, DC: United States Conference of Catholic Bishops, 1992.

Weddell, Sherry. *Forming Intentional Disciples: The Path to Knowing and Following Jesus*. Huntington, IN: Our Sunday Visitor, 2012.

———. *Fruitful Discipleship: Living the Mission of Jesus in the Church and in the World*. Huntington, IN: Our Sunday Visitor, 2017.

Winseman, Albert L. *Growing an Engaged Church: How to Stop "Doing Church" and Start Being the Church Again*. New York: Gallup Organization, 2006.

Chapter 3

Interactive Dialogue

Chapter 3 Preview

In this chapter, we will discuss the following:

- How to facilitate parish meetings that focus on action, not reports

- A *consent agenda* and how it improves meetings

- The critical role that *dialogue* plays in reaching consensus

- Understand *consensus* and how to announce it once it is reached

- How to practice communication skills such as *generative listening*

St. Michael's Parish—Making Better Meetings

Fr. Dave was preparing for another parish council meeting. He wondered, "*What is it about these meetings? Why do I dread them so much? I look forward to seeing the people but somehow the meetings go on forever and don't seem to get anything done.*"

Most parish council meetings are stuck in endless reports that could be read before people arrived. St. Michael's was no exception. The agenda was designed around committee reports that detailed past projects or advertised upcoming events that most people were already aware of.

Fr. Dave was interested in improving the quality of his parish council meetings. He was noticing that communication was going only in one direction. People joined the parish council with great enthusiasm, but after a few meetings, their interest waned. Attendance was down. The word on the street was that the meetings were just one boring report after another.

Ministry and Administration

"The Church is a business," a finance council member told Fr. Dave. "It should run more like a business." What he meant was that many churches needed to pay closer attention to matters of finance and administration.

Yes, there is a *business* side to the Church. A parish needs solid administration and efficient management by people authorized for those ministries. But the Church is first about ministry and then about administration.

This book is part of a series that includes books on finance, human resources management, and other administrative duties of a parish. This book is about the ministry of leadership, not the ministry of administration. As Pope Francis points out, *"Mere administration can no longer be enough. Throughout the world, let us be permanently in a state of mission."* Leadership and administration should both focus on mission.

The mission of the Church is its ministry.

THE BOTTOM LINE FOR THE CHURCH IS MISSION, NOT MONEY.

Yes, administration can be a form of that ministry. When we administer, we provide the *means* of support for all other ministry. Administration is the responsibility of those with the authority to administer. For example, churches need finance councils that provide good management to create the atmosphere, the structure, and the means for ministry and for leadership.

A mission statement has three components: (1) business, (2) purpose, and (3) values.

- The business of a parish is to *worship, serve, and form* Christians in the faith.

- The purpose of a parish is to *enable people to encounter Christ in their lives.*

- The core values are spelled out in Scripture, such as *faith, hope, and love.*

Every meeting, every action, every relationship, every commission, every prayer, and every form of business in a parish should contribute to the mission of the parish.

Church Meetings

One place the Church should *not* run more like a business is in its meetings. Plenty of business meetings go nowhere and do more to hurt relationships than to build a team. When the focus of a church meeting is *merely on administration*, as Pope Francis points out, it can lose sight of the overall mission. Meetings should advance the mission as the bottom line of the meeting.

One way to keep the focus on mission is to begin all meetings in the church with prayer and scriptural reflection. Prayer can remind us that we gather to do God's will, and to align our will collectively with God's will.

The Opening Prayer used at the Second Vatican Council is an example of how to start a meeting with prayer:

> We stand before you, Holy Spirit, conscious of our sinfulness, but aware that we gather in your name. Come to us, remain with us, and enlighten our hearts. Give us light and strength to know your will, to make it our own, and to live it in our lives.
>
> Guide us by your wisdom, support us by your power, for you are God, sharing the glory of Father and Son. You desire justice for all. Enable us to uphold the rights of others. Do not allow us to be misled by ignorance or corrupted by fear or favor. Unite us to yourself in the bond of love and keep us faithful to all that is true.

> As we gather in your name, may we temper justice with love, so that all our discussions and reflections may be pleasing to you, and earn the reward promised to good and faithful servants. We ask this of You who live and reign with the Father and the Son, one God, for ever and ever. Amen.

Church meetings are a time for the people of God to hold conversations about what is most *important* (and not just what is most *urgent*), to share their highest aspirations, to build relationships with each other, to confront the *reality* of their situation, to shape a new vision together, and to plan ways to put that vision into motion.

None of this will happen if our meetings focus on *telling* people what is happening, announcing what is going to happen, and approving perfunctory reports and statements. All reports should be written up, circulated, and read by each participant before the meeting. When we circulate a report in advance, and then we present it in the meeting, we encourage people *not* to read their reports. We penalize the people who do their homework.

FOCUS ON ACTION, NOT REPORTS.

Instead, **use a consent agenda**. Make one motion to approve all reports—including the minutes and agenda—all at once. Pause to see if there are any questions. Ask if anyone has an addition or change to the agenda. If not, move right into *action*. Focus on priority issues—based on the strategic pastoral planning that will be explained in chapter 5. This allows more time for the group to listen, dialogue, and make decisions that address critical issues instead of just hearing reports. It makes your meetings much more interesting, engaging, and productive.

Consensus

Action in a parish should be based on *consensus*. But what exactly does that mean? First, let's clarify what it is *not*. Consensus is *not* majority rule. It is *not* unanimity. It is *not* voting. Consensus does not mean that you move ahead when you get a vote of more than 50 percent. Nor does it mean you must get a vote of 100 percent.

Consensus means "the sense of the group." It is an agreement that transcends our usual way of deciding. Consensus occurs when

> a. everyone in the room has had a chance to express their views
>
> b. we have listened and understood each other
>
> c. we have summarized and expressed appreciation for all viewpoints, and
>
> d. everyone agrees that they can *at least live with* the decision to be made.

Consensus begins with a dialogue about the issue at hand. Everyone is encouraged to share their ideas. After all sides of the issue are discussed and explored, someone in the group, usually the facilitator, expresses what seems to be the emerging consensus. The wording of that consensus is tested and refined by group discussion. Then the facilitator asks, "Do we have consensus on this issue?" If even one person signals they are not ready, the dialogue continues.

One person may hold up consensus to clarify a question. Another might need more time to pray and reflect on a major decision. In some cases, one person might have a substantive disagreement. This

---

usually requires more time in dialogue, with more listening, summarizing, and conflict resolution skills we will discuss later.

Once everyone signals agreement, that is, *that everyone in the meeting can at least live with the decision*, the facilitator reiterates the content of the consensus for the sake of the minutes.

When you hold the *minority* viewpoint in a meeting to reach consensus, you should voice your concerns until you know they have been respected and understood. Once you have been heard, you should defer to the consensus. When you hold the *majority* viewpoint, your job is to show respect and demonstrate that you are listening and trying to understand the minority viewpoint(s). Only when you reach the point of mutual understanding and respect can people "agree to disagree" and move forward with the consensus.

CONSENSUS IS ABOUT VOICES, NOT VOTES.

Consensus is *not* governed by Robert's Rules. In fact, some of the worst meetings occur when experts in parliamentary law take over a meeting. While it is important to have structure in a meeting, and to vote on certain legal matters, Robert's Rules are more often used to manipulate than to nurture the will of the group.

Voting can enable those with positional power to enact change by majority rule. It is easier to settle a conflict by calling for a vote than to work toward consensus, but a split vote does not usually resolve the issue. Votes can cut off voices that need to be heard. Votes can hurt relationships. Consensus builds a team.

When we use Robert's Rules of Order and someone "calls the question," it gives one person the power to limit discussion for everyone else. It cuts off the movement toward consensus. Sometimes it does make sense to vote on technical issues such as logistics or financial reports. However, if you are deciding on issues of major importance, work toward consensus.

Voting in a parish might be necessary to record a decision for legal purposes. In this case, you can reach consensus and then formally vote on the consensus. Consensus is most appropriate for challenging issues, such as the following:

- *How can we* deepen our commitment to stewardship?
- *How can we* embrace full, active, and conscious participation in our liturgy?

Dialogue toward consensus will create a *shared vision* of the future of the parish. Pope Francis describes dialogue as a "search for the common good" and suggests that we need to be open to change through dialogue, as opposed to a "controlling, hard and prescriptive style."

Consensus is a decision-making process that is much more consistent with Church teaching because it strengthens our faith community. It is a catalyst for personal conversion. It enables the community to find common ground. As Brene Brown suggests, the consensus process puts our *vulnerability* on display by admitting that we do not have all the answers.

Discussion Question

How much time in your parish meetings is spent
- presenting and listening to reports?
- persuading people that someone already has the best solution?
- participating in a dialogue to solve real issues?

Dialogue

Consensus is reached through *dialogue*. It may take several meetings to reach consensus on difficult issues. It takes patience. It takes openness and willingness to change our minds and our actions, based on what we hear. In consensus, everyone has a voice that is shared.

Dialogue is a conversation in which people *think together*. Dialogue nurtures new insights. It challenges "how we usually do things around here." It questions our *tacit assumptions*, that is, those we may have taken for granted.

A dialogue is not the same as concurrent monologues. To think together, we focus our full attention on what the other person is saying instead of rehearsing what we will say in response. We postpone our preconceived notions of what the other person is going to say.

DIALOGUE IS THINKING TOGETHER.

Dialogue is a *conversation with a center*, not sides, according to William Isaacs. When our thoughts and emotions are in synch with each other, we reach a new center, with higher levels of reciprocal sharing. My idea tunes into your idea and together we come up with a better idea that neither of us could have developed on our own. No one takes credit for the idea.

Dialogue harnesses the collective energy of the team. It generates synergistic thinking together. It promotes collaborative solutions. Thinking, reflecting, and acting together improves relationships. In return, better relationships improve dialogue: The more we dialogue, the better our relationships. The better our relationships, the better our dialogue.

Dialogue is *countercultural*. In our individualist culture, we are more accustomed to thinking alone. The Greek word for *dialogue* means to "gather together" in search of new meaning. The Greeks understood this could only occur *collectively*. Dialogue is a conversation by people in relationship who are committed to search for a deeper sense of meaning.

Dialogue is *reciprocal*. The genuine climate of give and take is a mutual exchange that benefits each person. Dialogue is a multidirectional street. The conversation can include top-down, bottom-up, peer-to-peer, inside-out, and outside-in relationships.

Dialogue is *continuous*. The conversation may pause for prayerful reflection, or to try out some ideas, but the conversation comes back to revisit the ideas over and again. In some cases, a dialogue continues for months or years, such as a parish conversation about how to reach out to the unchurched and grow the parish.

Dialogue is *dialectic*. It brings divergent ideas and opinions together in a search for shared meaning. It is not about winners and losers, as in a debate. Each person (or each side) commits to reach a higher level of understanding. This can happen whenever we think, speak, and reason through a problem together.

DIALOGUE SEEKS THE COMMON INTEREST.

In a debate, we push for our own point of view while we resist what others are saying. To *debate* literally means to "beat down." The goal in a debate is to "convince," which literally means to "win." In a debate, we assume a zero-sum game. You win—and I lose. Or I win—and you lose. There is no win/win. Dialogue creates opportunities for collaboration.

Ironically, we often wish the other combatants would pay more attention to *us*. We see the other people as pushing their own point of view. The paradox here is that in most cases, both parties seem unaware that they are doing the same thing. They are treating others precisely the opposite way that they want to be treated. This is the *golden rule in reverse*. Both parties are doing to the other what they don't want the other to do to them.

Debate is a highly controlled conversation with both parties making their points, warding off attacks, competing for air time, attributing the worst of motives to the other side, advocating their own positions, and beating the other side down to reach a conclusion that is often unsatisfactory for both parties.

A dialogue can turn into a debate unless the leader is teaching and modeling the dialectic practice. It is all too natural for people to interrupt each other with knee-jerk reactions, instant responses, emotional outbursts, and other negative behaviors that limit our ability to dialogue.

Parish Activity

Select one of the following questions, both of which pose *false dichotomies*:

1. Which is more important: Completing the Task or Nurturing the Relationship?
2. Which is more important: Leadership or Management?

Put people into groups of three. Ask one person to present one side of the question while the second person summarizes what the first person has said and then checks with the first person to see if anything might be missing from the summary. Ask the second person to present the case for the other side of the question. Ask the first person to summarize what the second person said and check for accuracy. Then ask the third person to present the case as to why the answer to this false dichotomy is not *either/or* but *both/and*.

Four Practices for Healthy Dialogue

Isaacs shares four practices that are the building blocks for dialogue: (1) listening, (2) respecting, (3) suspending, and (4) voicing.

1. **Listening** is more than just hearing words. It is embracing and accepting what the other person is saying, intuiting the feelings behind the words, and reflecting on what is being expressed. Listening nurtures synergy.

2. **Respecting** means literally to "look again." Look again and see what we missed. Recognize the dignity of that human being. See that all people are created in God's image and likeness, that their thoughts and ideas deserve our consideration.

3. **Suspending** is withholding our judgment or holding back on forming a premature opinion. We suspend our opinion and open our minds to consider all options. When we form our opinion too soon—especially when we have publicly shared our opinion—we tend to defend our opinion and close our mind to the ideas of others.

4. **Voicing** is speaking our voice, sharing what we think, feel, and believe. It is crucial to hold off on speaking our voice too soon, for all the reasons above. It is especially

important to consider how the voice of the pastor or other persons in authority can affect everyone else in the room.

Another communication skill that is helpful for teachers and parents, and could be used by pastors and leaders, is to *deflect*. If someone else asks a good question, it can be tempting to answer it yourself. To *deflect* is to turn the question back to the group. Especially when the power distance is high between yourself and the rest of the group, it is important to understand that when the authority figure speaks up, it can end the conversation for some people. You might say, "That's a great question. What do others think?"

In a dialogue, we take turns. When one person finishes their response, everyone else has a choice: (a) to continue listening or (b) to assert their own thoughts, opinions, and positions. While you are listening, respecting, and suspending, it is hard to stay focused on what others are saying without *rehearsing* what you want to voice.

In a dialogue, we *deliberate*, which means to "weigh out," that is, to decide what you weigh as deeming your attention and what is not worth your attention. We deliberate every time we read the newspaper, sort through our e-mail, or listen to a colleague in a conversation.

In a dialogue, we deliberate between inquiry and advocacy: We *inquire* for more information or we *advocate* for a viewpoint (Isaacs). We shift between *asking and telling*.

How to Facilitate a Parish Meeting

To engage a parish council or committee in this type of dialogue will require skilled facilitation. The facilitator should not hold a position of authority over the group. It certainly should not be the pastor or a member of the parish staff. The person who is facilitating needs to devote her or his full attention to the personal dynamics in the room. This becomes impossible when the facilitator has a lot at stake or a lot to say.

If you are asked to facilitate a meeting, you need to operate at full capacity in all four areas of emotional intelligence: (1) be aware of your own emotions when the meeting gets testy; (2) be able to handle your own negative emotions; (3) be aware of the emotions of people around the room; and (4) be skilled in handling the emotions in the room.

Let's say you are facilitating a pastoral planning meeting at your parish. Here are some of the interactive dynamics you might be looking for—and interventions you might want to attempt:

- Do people *pause* long enough after a good question is asked—so that the reflective ones in the group have enough time to respond? If not, you might call on the quieter ones to give them a chance to talk.

- Are people using *eye contact* and nodding to the person who is speaking? If not, perhaps they are beginning to disengage. The facilitator might try to get the dialogue back on topic or get some new voices involved.

- Are participants beginning to *speak over* each other's voices? If so, you might want to ask the next two people that speak to restate what the previous person has said before making their own comment.

- Is anyone *dominating* the conversation while others are drifting away? If so, make a comment such as, "Thanks for sharing, Bill. Now let's hear what some of the others have to say about this."

- If two people begin speaking at the *same time*, what happens to the person who paused to allow the other to speak? Does she or he get lost in the rotation of speakers? If so, call on that person and ask if they have something to contribute.

- Is someone in the group getting edgy? Angry? Frustrated? Use a *reflective probe* to draw out that person. Make a comment such as, "You seem to be upset about this. Can you help us understand this from your perspective?"

- Are two or three people turning the dialogue into a *debate*? If so, ask each side to summarize what the other side has said. Then ask the other side to clarify anything that might be missing from the summary.

- Are people asking *loaded* questions, or *leading* questions, ones that suggest one right answer? If so, reframe the question as open-ended, such as, "How can we get this done? What are some of the options available to us?"

- Are people *showing empathy* toward others who have a viewpoint different than theirs? If not, you may have to make empathetic comments of your own. Say, "I get it." Or "I understand what you mean." Model the communication skills you want to see.

A facilitator must be able to read the emotions and hear the statements that are not necessarily being expressed out loud. Like the pitching coach of a baseball team who goes out to visit the pitcher's mound, we can't just sit in the dugout. To read how someone is doing, sometimes we have to ask them.

Please note: Even when you are not formally named as the facilitator, you can still help the quality and flow of a meeting by practicing any of the suggestions above. Let's say someone is trying to present an idea but someone else interrupts—and the facilitator does not say anything. Later, you might ask the person who was interrupted to finish presenting their idea. You could say, "Kathy, you didn't get a chance to finish what you were saying a few minutes ago. I'm curious, what else were you going to say?"

This is a simple act that *any* of us can take in any meeting. It can make everyone a bit more conscious about the group dynamics. It can reduce the number of interruptions, which are forceful ways to steal attention away from someone else. If left unchallenged, interruptions can become part of the culture of a group. They can become so habitual that they are hardly noticed. The key is to call them out before they become routine.

Generative Listening

In 1980, I was a young peace activist working for the Fellowship of Reconciliation (FOR) in New York. We were in our staff retreat and it came time for a break. I figured to quickly check the mail and phone messages. We didn't have smart phones. E-mail and text messages had not been invented yet.

The retreat was being led by Thich Nhat Hanh, the Vietnamese Buddhist who was an active member of the FOR. As I was running up the spiral staircase at the FOR headquarters, jumping two steps at a time, our retreat master was at the top of the stairs with his hand up, looking right at me.

"If you don't slow down, Dan," Thich Nhat Hanh told me, "I am going to spend the rest of this day walking mindfully up and down these stairs." Talk about life-giving advice. That moment often comes to mind when I am going too fast or trying to do too many things at once.

We all like to think that we can *multitask*. Neuroscience demonstrates that we have multitasked our brains into cognitive overload. This has depleted our ability to focus and made us less efficient, not more (Dimitriadis and Psychogios).

If one of the tasks we are attempting involves interacting with people, we need complete focus on that interaction. If I am listening or participating in a parish meeting, the interaction with other people requires my full, active, and conscious attention. If we are multitasking and one of the tasks is listening, we are probably missing something!

LISTENING IS A SOLO TASK.

The first step in listening is to "*be still*" (Ps 46:10). To still the noise inside our heads. A raging river does not allow us to see our image. Only when the water becomes still can we see ourselves in its reflection. In the same way, we can listen and reflect when we become still, when we create *still waters* within, that is, so we can reflect on what is inside us.

To be still is to separate ourselves from the noise. To silence our own thoughts so we can find our focus in a conversation. It is only when we are quiet that we can truly listen. Silence allows us to separate from the noise, so we can enter into the stillness of the Holy Spirit.

As the Dalai Lama suggests, focus does not mean we find *one* thing but that we shut out the *many* things. To be still helps us find our center: To shut out the past and the future so we can focus on the present. Thoughts about the argument we had this morning (the past) or the meeting that is coming up tonight (the future) are obstacles to living fully in the present. To listen, we must devote our full attention to the present.

Generative listening, according to Otto Scharmer, means to open (1) our minds, (2) our hearts, and (3) our will. First, we open our minds to deliberate on a new idea. Second, we open our hearts to identify with the emotional troubles of the other person. Third, we open our will to change the way we act—based on what we are hearing.

Let's say you have something important to discuss with your pastor. You see him right after Mass, perhaps at the front door or in the coffee room. If you want your pastor's full attention, it is probably not best to discuss something important right after Mass, when he is busy greeting people. Instead, mention that you will be calling him later in the week to set up an appointment. If you try to hold a conversation while he is distracted, you are inviting miscommunication.

Sometimes we listen to respond, or to judge, or to debate. We look for key words or phrases and assume the rest of what the other person will say. We launch into our own predetermined response. We talk over people. We cut them off. We are so eager to contribute ourselves that we close our ears. We lose our self-awareness and talk too much.

When we listen to learn, or to understand and gain the perspective of the other, we change the way we think and act. We shut out distractions. We pay attention to the nonverbals. We notice the emotions behind the words. We let people finish what they are saying. We encourage them by saying, "Tell me more about this" or "Help me understand that."

THE EYES MAY SEE, AND THE EARS MAY HEAR,

BUT UNDERSTANDING COMES FROM THE HEART

(SEE ISA 6:10; JER 5:21; EZEK 12:2; MATT 13:15; ACTS 28:27).

Generative Dialogue

Dialogue is a *listen-and-summarize-and-respond* cycle: You speak. I listen, I summarize, and I add my response. You listen, you summarize, and you respond. Others listen, summarize, and respond. The summary does not have to be long. It just acknowledges the prior response(s). This is how a group begins to *think together*. The listen-and-summarize-and-respond cycle lifts everyone to a higher understanding of the topic.

Leadership requires communication in multiple directions. The leader in the listen-and-summarize-and-respond cycle is just one voice—like anyone else. In fact, the role of leadership in a dialogue expands to virtually everyone, because each person is influencing and being influenced by others at various points in the cycle. This is what Joseph Rost means when he says that "leaders and followers do leadership together."

Generative dialogue occurs when we hear the message with an *open mind*. We hear the emotions behind the message with an *open heart*. We hear the message and the emotions with an *open will* to change our behavior. The change occurs in our thoughts, in our emotions, and ultimately in our actions.

GENERATIVE DIALOGUE MEANS OPEN MINDS, OPEN HEARTS, AND OPEN WILLS.

The biggest obstacles to generative dialogue are the distractions in our own heart and head. The two biggest impediments to living fully in the *present* are the past and the future. We are thinking and emoting about memories of the *past* or dreams of the *future*. We are thinking or emoting about the argument we had with our friend before the meeting or anticipating what we are going to cook for dinner tonight.

Let's say that Mike is voicing his concern about the lack of donations to our capital drive to build a new parish hall. Instead of listening closely to him, I think back to how Mike was telling me about his new car. I make a snap judgment on Mike's character and shut off listening to his ideas about the parish hall.

The memory of a previous conversation or a past negative experience we had with the one talking can easily distract us from the message. We can ruminate about the list of things we would rather be doing. We can pay too much attention to the past or the future.

Leadership is not a person but an activity that involves leaders and followers. Everyone practices leadership at some point in a generative dialogue, that is, when they take the initiative, step through the threshold of a new idea, and influence others in the dialogue. Leaders become followers and followers become leaders.

To be in a team dialogue means we listen to more than one person. We listen to discern the *collective* will of the whole group. A dialogue sets out to discover consensus. To practice leadership in a dialogue is to keep the focus on the emerging consensus.

Let's say you are in a parish council meeting. You are trying to discern a new direction. You have some strong ideas born of your own reflections. *Should you jump right in with your idea? Should you be the first to speak up?*

Look at it this way: If you jump right in, and another person sees things differently, there is little

---

chance that person is going to really listen to you. This is called low *receptivity*. People who have an opposing viewpoint will probably be rehearsing their own message, not yet ready to receive your message. You can increase the receptivity of other people if you listen to their idea first. It's human nature. People are more likely to listen to you when and if you have listened to them!

Listening during a dialogue does not mean simply staying quiet. Listening involves *mentally summarizing* what they are saying, *empathizing* with their emotional pain, and eventually *asking* the right questions. This discipline can help you reach *attunement*, which literally means you are "in tune" with the rest of the group. Attunement raises receptivity.

LISTEN FIRST. THEN SUMMARIZE AND RESPOND.

The most skillful leader in a dialogue knows how to listen patiently as others express their views, withhold judgment until a consensus begins to emerge, and then enter the dialogue by first summarizing what others are saying—preferably by quoting people *by name*—and then articulating the consensus.

When you have an opinion that is contrary to what is being said, enter the conversation skillfully by saying, "*I understand that you think that a Sunday Mass would be appealing to a young adult audience* (summary). *I appreciate your viewpoint* (affirmation). *I see it a bit differently...*(advocacy)."

Going Last

A few years ago, the Archdiocese of Dubuque asked me to facilitate two days of strategic planning—which can be a dialogue about the future. Before they contacted me, they had already drafted an agenda. The meeting was to begin with Archbishop Michael Jackels sharing his vision for the future of the archdiocese. When I saw this, I suggested that if the archbishop did this at the beginning of the first day, we might as well end the meeting right there. Most people would figure that the archbishop had already made up his mind about what needed to be done and would not be listening to what others had to say.

LEADERS GO LAST SO THEY CAN LISTEN, SUMMARIZE, AND BUILD CONSENSUS.

I respectfully asked the archbishop to hold off his comments until the end of the second day. He agreed. He participated in small groups but was careful not to dominate any conversations. He listened very carefully. That became clear when, at the end of the second day, he summarized what he had heard and articulated the vision as the consensus that had emerged from the group. He called out many of the participants by name as he summarized what he had heard. It was a powerful moment and the people went away feeling like they had been respected, consulted, and heard.

AS PETER DRUCKER PUT IT, "THINK FIRST, SPEAK LAST."

When we truly respect someone, we believe they have something to teach us, something we can learn if we take the time and give the energy needed to listen. When we listen, we respect the *dignity* of that human person.

Parish Activity

Let's say you want to set up a practice dialogue with your parish council or commission. Select a topic, such as, "How can we get more youth and young adults involved in our parish?" Put people into groups of four or five. Ask them to spend thirty minutes in dialogue about the question you select. Set specific procedures for this practice session, such as requiring that before anyone enters the conversation, they must first

 a. Summarize what the previous person has just said and

 b. Check with that previous speaker to see if they missed anything important.

When you apply these types of procedures, it forces people to listen more attentively. The human brain is not as likely to drift toward rehearsing what you are going to say when you know that you must first summarize what is being said.

After this practice, ask each group to report back some of the ideas that emerged out of the conversation. You may be surprised at the results.

When you find your group struggling with dialogue, go back to these procedures from time to time to reinforce the importance of listening.

Self-Talk at Your Meeting

Let's say you are chairing a commission for your parish. You are preparing to go to a parish council meeting. You just know you are about to engage in battle with Katie. Just the thought of spending two hours in the same room with Katie raises your anxiety. She is always personally attacking you. You ask yourself, *Who does she think she is anyway? Never a positive word. Always disagrees with whatever I suggest.*

You wonder, *Why do I have to attend these meetings anyway? Nothing ever gets accomplished. It's just a time for people from the parish to come together and gripe about what they don't like. And the meetings go on for hours. Why me? Why this?*

That morning in prayer, your mind keeps wandering to thoughts and feelings about this meeting. You find yourself praying for a change in Katie's behavior: *Lord, please let her be more positive. If she would just listen. If she would just give me some benefit of the doubt. After all, we are all in this parish together. Don't we all have the same goal in mind? Are we not trying to build your kingdom? Why can't she see that?*

Then it strikes you. Deep in prayer, it begins to dawn on you: *Maybe I should direct my prayers toward my own behavior.* But doubt enters again: *Why me? Why do I need to change? I haven't done anything wrong. I give my heart and soul to this parish. All I do is work.*

But as you continue to reflect on this meeting, another thought enters: *Maybe if I change my behavior, Katie might change hers.* You begin to consider this possibility. Your thoughts begin to shift toward Katie's perspective: *After all, wasn't that what the homily was about last weekend: more compassion, more empathy toward others?*

You consider anew the issue from Katie's perspective: *Maybe it's hard to be a woman in this parish. Especially one who is trying to initiate change. Maybe she is right. Maybe we need to consider some new ways of getting more people involved. We all know that it's the same people doing the same things all the time.*

But please, Lord, not Katie! She always has an ax to grind. She is one of those women who just wants to take over everything. Once I loosen my control of the commission, who knows where she will take things? Besides, she doesn't know how we do things around here. She has only been in this parish for a few years. She already thinks she owns the place.

On the other hand, maybe we need some new people to take some initiative around here. Heaven knows we have not been growing. Participation is down. The collection is down, and the same people are doing the same things. Maybe we need some new ideas.

You begin to shift your reflection toward your relationship with Katie. You begin to reflect more on her perspective as a young woman in a parish where the average age of the active parishioners is over sixty. You recall her ideas that might appeal to younger families and adults.

SELF-TALK CAN CHANGE THE NARRATIVE OF THE STORY YOU TELL YOURSELF.

Perhaps if I listen more and show some appreciation to Katie, maybe, just maybe, we could get more young people involved in the parish. Instead of praying for her to change, maybe I need to change. What if I were more positive, listened to her, and gave her the benefit of the doubt? Maybe that would change her behavior as well.

That night, when the meeting begins, Katie starts right into her usual antics. Right off, she criticizes the liturgy: "Why can't we have more young people involved? Why can't we update the music? Why do we always have to do things the same way we've done them before?"

Your blood pressure is rising. Your gut feels uneasy. *There she goes again.* But the goodwill that was built up in this morning's reflection takes the edge off your emotional reaction. *Patience, patience, just listen.* You take the time to listen. You even summarize some of what she said. You acknowledge her feelings of frustration. You consider her point of view and let her know that.

How different the rest of the meeting might go. How different Katie's behavior might be. If we start with changing our own behavior, we just might be able to change the reactions of others. Eventually, we begin to change the neurological patterns in our own brain and connect to our own heart. We might even change the culture of the meetings we struggle through.

Lectio Divina

Since the 1980s, I have used *Lectio Divina* at the beginning of most church meetings. It reminds all of us why we are gathered together. It informs our meetings with scriptural wisdom. And it nurtures relationships in the group. People enter into the rest of the meeting more prepared to dialogue.

There are several ways of doing *Lectio Divina* (see Appendix B). Many use the next Sunday's readings, along with an opening prayer, some reflection questions, and a closing prayer. Sr. Laura Goedken created such a handout for each Sunday for each liturgical year (see "Sharing Faith First" on the stewardship page of the Diocese of Davenport's website).

Whether you choose the next Sunday readings or not, *Lectio Divina* offers a meaningful way to dialogue about Scripture. Ask people to listen for whatever words or phrases seem to be calling out to them from the reading that day. Remember to begin each session with silence and allow time for people to share their thoughts, ideas, and prayers.

Trust and Collaboration

Dialogue is a way of thinking, reflecting, and conversing together so that your council or commission can find answers that none of them could have imagined by themselves. They find a deeper sense of shared meaning. They develop a mutual understanding of mission and vision, and they develop mutual relationships among themselves.

Dialogue can create a deeper and more active faith life. It can create a parish environment that enhances the faith life of the whole community, but none of this happens without the development of trust.

TRUST IS THE GLUE AND THE GREASE OF LEADERSHIP.

Leadership cannot exist without trust. Nor can engagement. Nor dialogue. Nor consensus. Trust is both the *glue* that holds everything together on a team and the *grease* that makes it all work.

To *collaborate* means to "work together." The more we collaborate, the more we trust. The more we trust, the more we collaborate. With trust and collaboration, we are either going through a *vicious cycle*, where both are declining in synch with each other, or a *virtuous cycle*, where both are growing in synch with each other.

Trust is *not* unconditional. It begins when you act *trustworthy*, which means you are *worthy of trust*. You act with *integrity*, which means that you *integrate* your values and your behaviors. You practice what you preach. You do what you say. Acting with integrity is the most important thing you can do to get into the virtuous cycle with trust.

To get others to act as trustworthy is not within your control. However, you can encourage people to spend more time together. Encourage them to build relationships. Set aside time in your meetings for people to get to know each other. Like the two teams that become one in the movie *Remember the Titans*, sometimes we need to just spend time together. Even when it feels like a waste of time, it can build the positive connection between trust and collaboration.

It takes a lot of trust, commitment, and cohesion to engage in meaningful dialogue. Like the soil in the parable of the sower (Matt 13:1–23), the soil of our parishes must be nurtured with trust in order to be prepared for collaboration. This can allow the garden of leadership to see the sunlight and be nurtured into new growth.

Chapter Summary

In this chapter, we covered the *interactive people skills*, such as facilitation, listening, and dialogue, that can enhance your relationships and effectiveness as a leader. Our meetings would be much more productive if we took the time to practice the mindful, heartful ways of generative dialogue.

The next chapter takes a closer look at *adaptive challenges*—the ones for which there are no easy answers. Adaptive leadership is likely to generate plenty of conflict. The key is to stimulate *task conflict* without letting it escalate into *relationship conflict*.

References

Bohm, David. *On Dialogue*. New York: Routledge, 1996.

Brown, Brene. *The Power of Vulnerability: Teachings on Authenticity, Connection, and Courage*. Louisville, CO: Sounds True Publishing, 2012.

Collins, Jim. *Good to Great and the Social Sectors: A Monograph to Accompany Good to Great*. Boulder, CO: Jim Collins, 2005.

Dalai Lama. *How to Practice: The Way to a Meaningful Life*. New York: Atria Books, 2002.

Davidson, Richard J., and Sharon Begley. *The Emotional Life of Your Brain*. New York: Hudson Street Press, 2012.

Dimitriadis, Nikolaos, and Alexandros Psychogios, A. *Neuroscience for Leaders: A Brain-Adaptive Approach*. London: Kogan Page Unlimited, 2016.

Goleman, Daniel. *Emotional Intelligence*. New York: Bantam Dell, 2005.

Isaacs, William. *Dialogue and the Art of Thinking Together: A Pioneering Approach to Communicating in Business and in Life*. New York: Doubleday, 1999.

Marquardt, Michael J. *Leading with Questions: How Leaders Find the Right Solutions by Knowing What to Ask*. San Francisco: Jossey-Bass, 2014.

Pope Francis. *The Joy of the Gospel (Evangelii Gaudium)*. Rome: Libreria Editrice Vaticana, 2013.

Pope Francis. "Catholics Must Be Open to Change," *Vatican Correspondent*, November 10, 2015.

Scharmer, Otto, and Katrin Kaufer. *Leading from the Emerging Future: From Ego-System to Eco-System Economies; Applying Theory U to Transforming Business, Society, and Self*. San Francisco: Berrett-Koehler Publishers, 2013.

Chapter 4

Leading Adaptive Change

Chapter 4 Preview

In this chapter, Fr. Dave will explore the following:

- What *adaptive challenges* are facing the Church
- How to lead *adaptive change*
- The difference between leading and managing change
- A *three-step meeting* to lead through conflict
- Various types and approaches to conflict

St. Michael's—Working toward Change

Fr. Dave acknowledged that St. Michael's needed change. The parish needed to expand activities for the youth, step up their efforts to increase participation of young adults and young families, and strengthen their adult faith formation programs. That would be a start.

St. Michael's needed more lay leadership and a deeper sense of lay engagement. Fr. Dave hungered for more active and conscious participation in the liturgy. He yearned for spiritual growth among his parishioners. He knew that St. Michael's could be a more welcoming congregation. He longed to establish a clearer sense of mission and vision in the parish.

The parish had many leadership challenges. In a word, the parish needed change.

In this chapter, we will discuss how parishes need systemic change, such as a change of culture and structure. This requires a change of attitude and behavior. It is what Ronald Heifetz calls *adaptive change*. Parishes also need some immediate improvements that he calls *technical fixes*. What they don't need are technical fixes applied to adaptive challenges.

Leading adaptive change will inevitably involve conflict. Part of leading adaptive change is to encourage the hearts and excite the minds of the people so they are not comfortable with the status quo. The key is to inspire differences of opinion about what needs to be done, without allowing those honest differences to escalate into relationship conflict.

Change

Change is at the heart of leadership. If you are not changing something, you are not leading. You might be managing, administering, or fixing something, but *it is not leadership unless it involves change.*

LEADERSHIP REQUIRES CHANGE.

Scripture talks about change in terms of new beginnings, awakenings, creation, conversion, renewal, reconciliation, transformation, and building the kingdom of God.

As Dorothy Day pointed out, "What we would like to do is change the world—make it a little simpler for people to feed, clothe, and shelter themselves as God intended for them to do." Dorothy taught us that we could change the world by changing the little things, one step at a time. She was actively involved in providing hospitality for the poor while always maintaining her activism for social change.

A *Kairos* Moment

Imagine coming home from work one day and your spouse tells you, "I want you to come to the orphanage tomorrow to meet your son!" This happened to my friend Miguel Santos. His wife, Myra, was working at an orphanage in Mexico. She had fallen in love with an infant whose health was failing. Miguel says he initially thought, "This is no time for me to be a father."

Miguel was thinking in *chronos time*, which is chronological time, or *our time*. His wife was realizing a *kairos moment*, which is *God's time*. God was calling Miguel and Myra to adopt this infant, who was to become their son, Antonio Salvador. As God's people, we are always challenged to discern God's version of what is timely.

The change that Jesus creates is change in *kairos* time. It is breaking news, created in God's time, not ours. For some, the good news is a rude awakening. Jesus said he did "not come to bring peace, but a sword" (Matt 10:34), meaning he was seeking change, not harmony. Many saw Jesus as a trouble-maker. It was a good trouble, but it was trouble.

Scholars talk about change as adjustments, adaptations, transactions, amendments, modifications, reforms, transformation, and revolution.

The change that we are creating may sometimes occur in *chronos* time. In fact, it can seem like a glacial process. It may seem to take forever. It requires patience to break through the bureaucracy. It takes wisdom to discern solutions. And it takes courage to seize the opportunities for change in the Church. Yet change we must.

CHANGE OUTSIDE REQUIRES CHANGE INSIDE.

Without change, our parishes will die. The principle of *entropy* suggests that every living thing is in the process of dying. Unless we breathe new life into our parishes, they too will die. The outside world is changing, and unless we adapt to the changes in that world, our organizations will die.

Imagine a parish that has yet to adapt to the changes brought on by social forces like globalization, immigration, consumerism, and individualism, or technological changes such as the internet, computers, or cell phones. These parishes are no longer alive.

An adaptive organization is one designed to evolve. It aligns itself with its constantly changing environment. It is responsive and fluid. It creates an organic connection to the community it serves. It becomes resilient. Our parishes need to become adaptive and resilient.

Leading Change

To adapt is to change, to adjust to the times. Adaptive change begins with discernment, with reading the signs of the times—the signs in both *chronos* and *kairos* time. Within that discernment, there is the question of God's will. What is the *kairos* moment telling us? To what kind of change is God calling us? How can we align our will with the will of God?

Once we answer that question, we can devote our minds, our hearts, and our will to lead that change. We look to the *chronos* changes in our world and our community. We ask people inside and outside the parish to identify with us the most important trends that are affecting our parish life (see chapter 5).

Chronos time waits for no one. If you are not changing for the better, you are probably getting worse. The law of entropy applies to every plant, every animal, and every organization. Resistance to change is folly. Change is constant. Throughout the universe. To ignore the change occurring *outside* your parish is to risk decline in stewardship, participation, and engagement *inside* your parish.

Leaders stimulate change. If your parish keeps doing the same thing in the same way with the same people, it is losing ground to entropic forces. Without adapting to the changing times, how will we see growth in spiritual vitality, stewardship, and evangelization? More lively participation at Mass? More active outreach into the community? More dialogue and fewer boring meetings? How can we expect people to be *engaged as missionary disciples of Christ*?

Unless we are willing to generate some newness, we will continue to get the same results we have always gotten. The scribes and the Pharisees wanted the status quo. They just wanted everyone to follow the rules. Jesus challenged them to form new hearts and new minds committed to a new covenant (Matt 26:28). Jesus challenged the status quo (Matt 23).

Leading change is living on a threshold. Leadership thrives on the doorstep of change. Margaret Wheatley says that leaders dwell in that part of the world where the old is giving way to the new. Leaders see with eyes that listen. They hear with ears that see. They feel with hearts that bleed for those who are suffering. As Robert F. Kennedy once stated, leaders imagine things that might be and ask, *Why not*?

CHANGE IS THE STUFF OF LEADERSHIP.

Leaders create space for change. They gather the people together to prayerfully listen with attentive hearts and thoughtful minds. They reflect and dialogue to harness the synergy of the collective wisdom of the group. They discern the will of God and then commit themselves wholeheartedly to that change.

Adaptive versus *Technical*

Ronald Heifetz was a medical doctor. He coined the term *adaptive challenge* based on reflecting on his medical practice. Patients search for easy solutions to their health problems. They often stop there. They want their doctor to make their medical problems just go away: "Take this drug and your symptoms go away." "Get this laminectomy and your back problems go away." Heifetz saw that patients were unwilling to change their own daily habits, even when those habits were the cause, or at least an aggravation, of their medical condition. The same can be said for parishes. We often look for the quick answer, the easy solution.

Adaptive issues require more analysis, research, and discussion. They require a change in attitude, behavior, or values. If you have a cold, you may need to change your diet, schedule, and routines. If you have a bad back, you may need to change the way you lift, what you carry, and how long you sit.

ADAPTIVE LEADERSHIP CHANGES HEARTS AND MINDS.

A technical fix is a known solution. Most problems have technical and adaptive aspects. Let's say you have lower back surgery. That may solve a technical issue in your lumbar system. But if you are unwilling to do the physical therapy, and change some of your daily habits, your back problem will resurface.

Let's say you have a flat tire. You repair the tire. That is the technical fix. Your problem may be solved. However, if you have another flat tire the next day, and the next, you should look for the cause of the flat tires. Maybe you have roofing nails on your driveway. The adaptive approach looks more systemically at the problem.

Let's consider the idea of building a wall on the Mexican border. When I talked to people in the Rio Grande Valley, even the most ardent supporters of border security said that the wall would not fix the issue of immigration. At best, it is a technical fix to an adaptive problem. The adaptive challenge is to address the social, economic, and human causes that explain *why* so many Mexicans want and need to cross the border.

A technical fix works *when and if* the problem is technical. In the same way that injustice demands more than charity alone, adaptive challenges require more than a technical fix. Adaptive change requires a change of *hearts and minds*.

Adaptive challenges in a parish might pose the following questions:

- How can we live as faithful stewards of God's gifts?
- How can we engage the hearts and minds of our youth and young families?
- How can we fully, actively, and consciously participate in the liturgy?
- How can we share the light of God's love to the unchurched?
- How can we convert our hearts and minds to the pursuit of social justice?
- How can we transform our neighborhoods and communities?

Discussion Question

What are the adaptive challenges facing your parish?

Social Justice as an Adaptive Challenge

Fr. Marv Mottet grew up during the Depression. His father delivered milk. When families could not afford the milk, Marv's father delivered it anyway. Sometimes he bartered for payment. Sometimes he just donated the milk. Somehow, Marv said, there was always food on the table. Marv's father taught him that God will provide to those who do God's work.

When Fr. Marv became national director of the Catholic Campaign for Human Development (CCHD), he was essentially the CEO of a multimillion dollar organization. He could have lived in a palace. Instead, he chose to start a Catholic Worker House and live with the homeless. He slept on a mattress on the floor. When I visited Marv during those years, I discovered that he was living in one of the worst neighborhoods in Washington, DC.

Fr. Marv's life was dedicated to living and working with the poor. When he was the social action director for the Diocese of Davenport, he created his Two-Feet Model of Social Action: Charity and Justice. "It takes both feet," he said, "to walk the walk." His "two feet" approach is now used all over the country as a model for social change.

When he returned to Davenport after seven years with CCHD, Fr. Marv became my pastor. He was rector of Sacred Heart Cathedral, where he got personally involved in revitalizing the surrounding low-income neighborhood. What I remember most about Marv as pastor is that he was *invitational*. When he needed something, he would ask. He was always inviting me, and many others, to do something.

When I became social action director for the Diocese of Davenport, Fr. Marv schooled me almost daily in the practice of maintaining balance between charity and justice. One day, he would call about a family in need. The next day it was a social justice issue. He believed in starting each day with the newspaper in one hand and the Bible in the other.

IT TAKES BOTH FEET TO WALK: CHARITY AND JUSTICE.

Fr. Marv knew that to create lasting social change, you need to get at the causes of poverty and injustice. He addressed poverty as an adaptive challenge. He also knew that the Christian life involves living, serving, and working among the poor.

The adaptive challenge for the social activist is to engage in both charity and justice.

Going the Second Mile

On a missionary trip to El Salvador in 1986, I had the opportunity to visit with Archbishop Rivera y Damas. He was the successor to Archbishop Oscar Romero, the beatified martyr and beloved leader of the people of El Salvador.

The reading for that day was from the Sermon on the Mount: "If anyone forces you to go one mile, go also the second mile" (Matt 5:41). Archbishop Rivera y Damas told us that day that coming to El Salvador was our first mile. Our second mile, he said, was to return home and work for an end to the civil war and systematic oppression in El Salvador.

That first mile was what Fr. Marv would call the *work of charity*. Our second mile was the *work of justice*. Too often, we stop after the first mile. We walk on one foot, the foot of charity. We walk back and forth along the path of that first mile. The second mile is adaptive work. It is unfamiliar territory for many parishes. The work is hard. It can be controversial.

Let's say that you are leading your parish social action commission. You are in a poor neighborhood where many people have difficulty paying their bills. A technical solution might be to raise money for direct financial assistance. Charity is the first step. Every parish needs to be charitable. But it takes more than one foot to walk.

The second step is social justice. This is where we engage the adaptive aspect of social action ministry. As with all adaptive issues, it is critical to involve the people most affected by the problem in the search for adaptive solutions. That is why most congregations should be involved in church-based community organizing, such as those funded by CCHD.

Similarly, Catholic Relief Services (CRS) works to solve adaptive challenges in an international context. Support for CRS, especially its Rice Bowl program, is critical to any parish that wants to address the adaptive challenges posed by global poverty.

We tend to apply technical fixes to adaptive problems. And stop there. We default to what is easy, what we already know. We struggle with adaptive challenges.

Discussion Question

To what adaptive challenges are you trying to apply
a technical fix in your parish?

Stewardship as an Adaptive Challenge

Let's say your finance council decides to increase your parish offertory. The adaptive side of this challenge will be to ask people to change their attitudes, behaviors, and beliefs about their money. Recall the story about the pastor who was announcing a fund drive to his parishioners and said, "I've got good news and sad news....The good news is we already have all the money we need. The sad news is that it is still in your pockets."

Stewardship begins with a conversion of the heart, recognizing all as gift and all gifts as inherited from God. The generous heart gives cheerfully (2 Cor 9:7). The adaptive challenge in stewardship is converting hearts and minds to be grateful for what we have instead of feeling entitled to more. Reflecting on gratitude can be a counterbalance to the culture of entitlement that can consume us. This is an adaptive change for those in stewardship ministry.

STEWARDSHIP IS AN ADAPTIVE CHANGE IN THE HEART.

A technical fix with a campaign to increase the parish offertory might be as simple as increasing the number of parishioners who give electronically every week. People who donate directly through a bank deposit are more generous, reliable, and consistent givers. This is low-hanging fruit for a campaign to increase offertory giving. But alone it will not solve much.

Consider the example of the Diocese of Wichita. They took a plunge into stewardship several decades ago. In all parishes, people began to tithe 10 percent of their income. The diocese flourished. Parishes found resources to do ministry. Schools offered free tuition. However, it was not as simple as saying, "Everyone will now tithe 10 percent of their income to the parish, and we will offer free Catholic school tuition." It was an adaptive leadership effort by Msgr. Thomas McGread and many others. It required a conversion of hearts and minds.

Many people wish that their pastor or bishop would "decree" stewardship and make it happen. They figure that people in authority should command the change. They do not realize that adaptive work requires a deeper, personal change that cannot be dictated. In fact, to become a stewardship parish requires a change in the very *culture* of the church community. Free school tuition will be the *fruit* of adaptive change, not the *cause*. There is no technical fix that will engage the hearts and minds of the people in stewardship.

Rules can be used as a technical fix to adaptive problems. Take Sunday obligation for example. We can guilt people into going to Mass. What does that really change? How can we find intrinsic ways of motivating people to attend Mass voluntarily? How do we get laypeople to appreciate the Mass as the source and summit of all graces? How do we inspire people to see their relationship with Christ as the center of their lives?

WE TEND TO APPLY A TECHNICAL FIX TO ADAPTIVE PROBLEMS.

Traveling to the main square in Pristina, the capital of Kosovo, I was struck by how many signs stated that it was against the law to litter. Yet there was litter everywhere. We saw hired hands with trash pickers walking the streets. But the technical fixes were not working. The rules were not being followed. Littering seemed to be engrained in the culture.

A student of mine tells the story of his daughter who wanted to be married in a Catholic parish but was not a practicing Catholic. His daughter called his parish. The receptionist heard her story and informed her she could not get married there because she was not practicing her Catholic faith. She asked to talk to a priest. The receptionist said, "No, the priest will tell you the same thing."

My student, a practicing Catholic, called the parish. He got the same result. His daughter got married elsewhere, her parents left the parish, and no one in the family practices the Catholic faith any longer—due to strict adherence to the rules without any room for dialogue.

JESUS WANTS US TO ENGAGE HEARTS AND NOT JUST APPLY THE RULES.

On the other hand, some parishes see phone calls like these as an opportunity for evangelization. Instead of strict adherence to the law, they sit down and talk face-to-face to young couples who are looking for a place to get married. They invite them to become active members of the parish. They engage in a dialogue, not a monologue.

Rule-making is a form of legalism. Rules do not change people's hearts or minds. They might even encourage resistance to change. Jesus spoke out strongly against the legalism of the scribes and Pharisees (Matt 23). He set out to change hearts and minds—not to establish a new set of rules that would be applied as a technical fix.

Adaptive Strategies

Heifetz, Grashow, and Linsky (2014) put it this way: "Adaptive work requires a change in values, beliefs, or behavior." The process they lay out is simple: adaptive leadership is an iterative process involving three key activities:

1. Observe the events around you.

2. Interpret what you observe.

3. Design an intervention.

Each of these activities builds on the one that comes before it. First, we use our five senses to sense what is happening around us. Second, we practice mindful and heartful analysis of the situation. Third, we discern our strategy.

For Catholics, this process is similar to "See, Judge, Act," the inductive form of analysis prominent in Catholic social teaching, such as *Mater et Magistra*. As in Catholic teaching, the scholars teach that the adaptive process is cyclical. You continue to refine your observations, interpretations, and interventions. You continue to see, judge, and act. It is an iterative process that is informed by trial and error.

Let's look at Heifetz and Linsky's steps to leading adaptive change.

1. Get on the Balcony

Getting on the balcony means to step back, see the reality of what is happening and reflect on what is really going on. The key is that as you imagine yourself looking from the balcony, you can see yourself and others objectively on the stage floor. You observe yourself in interaction with others and admit the mistakes you might be making.

This requires both *self*-awareness and *social* awareness. When you get on the balcony, your observations about your actions and their reactions will only ring true if you act with the emotional and social intelligence discussed earlier. When you do, such a view from the balcony can provide the bigger picture. This becomes even more important during the heat of action.

In Catholic teaching, we might call this *contemplative action*. The pastoral planning cycle invites us to balance pastoral action with prayerful reflection. We get into trouble when we go from one activity to the next without taking time to breathe.

PERSONAL CONVERSION BEGINS WITH SELF-AWARENESS.

---

2. Think Politically

The second strategy in adaptive leadership is to reflect on power and interests. *Power* is defined here simply as the "ability to act." Power is neither positive nor negative, although it can be used as a means toward positive or negative ends.

According to French and Raven, the source of the power may be: (a) formal, such as the ability to reward or to punish, which comes from a position of authority; or (b) informal, such as character, reputation, and relationships, which comes from the person.

Power is necessary to enact any change. It is a means to an end. When sought as an end unto itself, power is viewed as negative. Seeking power as an end unto itself is the opposite of servant leadership, where the primary motivation is "not to be served but to serve" (Matt 20:28). However, without power, there is no leadership. That includes servant leadership, where power is harnessed for the service of others.

Like power, the concept of *self-interest* tends to be viewed negatively. It sounds selfish to have self-interest. Yet we all have self-interest—whether we admit it or not. Self-interest simply answers, "What's in this for me?" Being clear about our self-interest is healthy. It is not selfish to recognize or to pursue self-interest, as long as you are able to recognize and pursue the interests of others in the process.

The adaptive leader becomes aware of self-interest in all parties. Awareness of interests is the basis for collaboration. A collaborative dialogue searches for a solution that meets the needs and interests of all parties.

KNOWING SELF-INTEREST IS KNOWING YOURSELF AMONG OTHERS.

To reach collaboration, we need to become assertive about our own interests and supportive of the interests of others. If I am not assertive about my interests, I am not giving you an opportunity to support my interests. And if I am not aware of your interests, I cannot cooperate on your interests.

Let's say that the evangelization committee wants to hold a retreat for young adults. They have spent months in dialogue and discernment to reach this consensus. Now they need to go to the finance council to present their idea and get financial support. Thinking politically means figuring out what are the needs and interests of the finance council.

A finance council is given the responsibility to be fiduciary stewards of the parish finances. Before going to the finance council, think about how you can make your request so it will meet their fiduciary interests. How much do you really need? How will you use the funds? How will you contribute to it yourselves?

A finance council also cares about the pastoral life of the parish. You should frame your message according to those interests. For example, bring some young adults with you to make the presentation. Ask them to share how this retreat will be aligned with the parish mission and vision. This will help you find a collaborative solution that meets the interests of the finance council and the young adults.

3. Orchestrate the Conflict

A precious diamond does not glitter until it is cut. A seed does not bear fruit until it has been planted in the ground and dies. In the same way, change can be painful. Adaptive issues need to be cut into manageable pieces.

Change usually involves some loss, but like the diamond that needs to be cut and the seed that needs to die, most change requires a willingness to take risks and make sacrifices. In fact, the extent of the risk is usually proportionate to the depth of the change and the extent of the learning involved, thus increasing the extent of the resistance.

Orchestrating the conflict is like holding your hand on the thermostat of change. At times, you need to turn up the heat to create more of a sense of urgency about the change. At other times, you need to turn the heat down, so you do not burn out your people. When leading change, you must be able to read the emotions in the room (social awareness) so you will know when to turn the heat up or down.

To increase the sense of urgency for change, according to John Kotter, is to "bring the outside world in." For example, if you are asking people to introduce more modern music into the liturgy, you might remind them of how urgent it is to attract more young families into the parish. If you are trying to introduce more of the Spanish language on to the parish website, you might want to document how many Latinos are in your neighborhood.

Without a sense of urgency, people lose heart. They can feel lazy and lethargic. With *too much* of a sense of urgency, people can also lose heart. They can feel overwhelmed and afraid. They can burn out. To decrease the sense of urgency, give people some time off. Take time for more prayer and reflection.

In either case—too much or not enough urgency—the people will resist change. Most resistance to change is resistance to loss. People resist loss. When you are the change agent, you need to (1) ask yourself what you are asking people to give up; (2) reach out to listen to the people with the most to lose; (3) prepare people to experience some loss before they see gains; and (4) remind people of why the change is necessary and what the gains will be.

If (a) the extent of dissatisfaction with the adaptive problem, is greater than (b) the extent of the loss you are asking people to endure, then (c) the extent of the resistance to change will weaken. Use this formula to determine the level of risk and sacrifice that can be tolerated.

PEOPLE RESIST THE CHANGE THEY DON'T CHOOSE.

When they choose the change, they buy into it. Adaptive leaders involve as many people as possible in the process of choosing the change. Then they find noncoercive ways to sell the idea to the masses. As the people buy into the change, resistance will weaken.

4. Give the Work Back

Today's adaptive challenges are too complex to be managed by rules or led by one person in authority, however competent that person might be. To apply adaptive solutions, we must involve the people closest to the problem and apply the collective wisdom of the group. For example, if you are addressing the adaptive challenges of families with small children, involve those young families in prayerful discernment and dialogue.

For example, you might think that the most important support you could provide young families is to offer childcare during Mass. Indeed, that might be helpful. On the other hand, the young parents might prefer to stay with their young children during Mass. You need to *ask* them. And then put them in charge of the issue. Give the work to them.

Your job as an adaptive leader is not to do the work or to solve the problem. Doers are not necessarily leaders. Doing something, especially by yourself, can be the antithesis of leadership.

LEADING IS NOT DOING THINGS BY YOURSELF.

Your job is to facilitate a process whereby your parish team enters into dialogue with the people who are closest to the problem to find the best solutions and strategies. In the best-case scenario, the dialogue reaches the synergy we discussed in previous chapters, that is, the team discovers a solution that none of them could have imagined by themselves.

In the adaptive leadership paradigm, leaders become followers and vice versa. They collaborate and remain in dialogue about where they are going and how to get there. Their roles constantly interchange as they seek to influence one another toward the intended change and the mutual purpose.

5. Hold Steady

Some of the biggest tragedies in history occurred when people with knowledge of the problem were too afraid to speak up. Think of the sinking of the Titanic and the explosion of the Challenger. Think of the clergy sexual misconduct scandals.

In adaptive leadership, those in authority build trust so that people who see a problem will speak up. They share their power *with* their direct reports instead of wielding power *over* them. Remember that the key to leading when you have authority is to resist the temptation to rely so heavily on that authority. When you are wielding your authority, you are not leading.

Leadership is an opportunity that presents itself daily. No one can make you a leader. A bishop can make you a pastor. A pastor can appoint you as a lay trustee. But to be a leader, you must seize the opportunity. Only you can decide whether you lead or not.

My parish has started tracking the ways that the general public comes into contact with the parish. It might be a phone call, an email, or a knock on the door. The request might be financial assistance, a funeral planning, or a wedding. It might be a neighborhood couple that has started a family and wants to baptize their child.

Many of these callers have had little or no involvement in any parish growing up. They find themselves needing the Church. It might be the first time they see the need for God in their lives. For the people answering these calls, they could be viewed as an interruption from their busy lives.

Like the story above, let's say that the caller wants to be married in the Church but has not practiced the Catholic faith since they were a small child. It would be easy to see this as a technical issue and tell the caller that the rules do not allow them to be married in the Church.

Instead of seeing these calls as inopportune distractions from their daily routines, my parish is viewing the calls as *on-ramp* opportunities for evangelization. The parish staff meets regularly to pray, dialogue, and discern a new direction for handling each of these calls. They view these public contacts not as problems but as opportunities. They approach each call as a unique opportunity to reach out to people in the neighborhood.

They are living out this call from Pope Francis: "Instead of being just a Church that welcomes and receives by keeping the doors open, let us try also to be a Church that finds new roads, that is able to step outside itself and go to those who do not attend Mass, to those who have quit or are indifferent. The ones who quit sometimes do it for reasons that, if properly understood and assessed, can lead to a return. But that takes audacity and courage."

A colleague of mine, Dave Krupke, says, "When you change the way you look at things, the things you look at change." When my parish began to look at these "on-ramps"—the ways that people call upon them—they discovered a new world of opportunity for evangelization.

Discussion Question

What are some strategies your parish could employ to address your adaptive challenges?

Managing Change

So far, we have been discussing the idea of *leading change*—that which is initiated through leadership. What happens when the change is mandated from the outside? What happens when it is dictated by the government or the diocese? When the forces calling for change are outside entities, and not the people themselves, then the pastor, deacon, parish staff, and others in authority are called upon to *manage the change*.

According to Heifetz and Linsky, people look to those in authority for three things: (1) protection, (2) direction, and (3) order. When change is mandated from the outside, those in authority are expected to (1) protect the interests of the parish, (2) provide direction for the change, and (3) reestablish order, despite the change that is being mandated from someone else.

If you are in a position of authority, and you are managing change that is coming from the outside, Heifetz and Linsky suggest these four steps:

1. Ask yourself what you are asking the people to give up.

2. Listen to the people with the most to lose.

3. Prepare them to experience some loss before they see gains.

4. Explain *why* the change is necessary and what the gains will be.

Let's say you are a member of the parish council and one of your big events each year is a fall festival that provides an opportunity for parish socializing. It gives ministries a chance to market themselves, and in the process, it raises lots of money. Your parish insurance company has just informed you of new policies that will restrict your ability to sell alcohol at the annual festival. You are certain that this ruling will limit the funds that the event will raise.

Your efforts to respond to this challenge are called *change management*. The change is being mandated from the outside. Your job is to manage that change by listening to the people with the most to lose and preparing them to adapt to the necessary change. Explaining *why* change is necessary will help to overcome the sense of loss and decrease the resistance to change. As Frederick Nietzsche once said, "He who has a *why* can endure any *how*." Explain why the insurance company had to make this change.

Leading through Conflict

Like change, conflict is inevitable. Leading change will certainly generate conflict. Conflict happens. It is a daily occurrence for people in relationship.

The key to conflict is to recognize it, embrace it, deal with it, and learn from it. When we take time to reflect on what happened, and we are open to recognizing our mistakes, we can see each conflict as an *opportunity* for improvement. Each day brings new conflicts. Each new conflict brings new opportunities to improve our conflict skills.

Learn from the past. Live the present. Yesterday is over. This is today. Your new opportunity begins with each new morning. Focus on the opportunity of today.

People in congregations often feel that conflict is a failure to love, forgive, and care for each other. Scripture reveals that conflict was present in the early Church. The Gospels (Matt 18:15–17; 23), the Acts of the Apostles (Acts 6:1–7; 15), and the epistles of St. Paul (Gal 2:12–13; 6:1; Rom 11:17–18), and St. James (Jas 4:1–12) demonstrate that even in a Christian community, there will be conflict.

Research by Karen Jehn (and many others) shows that small to moderate amounts of *task conflict* are healthy for teams and organizations. Task conflict simply means that you and I have a different approach to a task. We see the problem differently. Without task conflict, we lack the full range of perspectives we usually need to creatively solve a problem. Worse yet, we can have *groupthink*, which means everyone in the group is thinking the same way.

CONFLICT IS AN OPPORTUNITY TO CHANGE.

The Jehn research also shows that even tiny amounts of *relationship conflict* are unhealthy for teams and organizations. Relationship conflict occurs when we begin to attack each other instead of attacking the problem. Relational conflict needs to be addressed. Without attention, it tends to escalate.

One way to deal in a healthy way with conflict is to *normalize* it. Simply admit the fact that conflict occurs in every organization. It is *normal*. It is a daily experience for all of us. It happens to everyone, every day. Imagine how boring a movie, a novel, or any story would be without any conflict. It is the stuff of life. The key is to deal with it as task conflict before it escalates into relationship conflict.

Five Approaches to Conflict

Kenneth Thomas presents five approaches to conflict, based on how assertive you are about meeting your own interests (concern for the task), and how cooperative you are in helping the other person in the conflict meet their interests (concern for the relationship). The five responses to conflict line up along the same horizontal and vertical axes as the Q1, Q2, Q3, and Q4 model from chapter three (see chart on the next page).

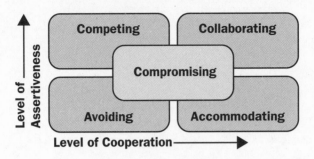

Five Conflict Handling Styles

When we *compete* (Q1), the goal is to win, to defeat the other parties to the conflict, to convince others that you are right and they are wrong. Given the competitive nature of our society, this is the most familiar reaction to conflict, especially by those in positions of authority.

When we *accommodate* (Q3), the goal is to let the other person get whatever they want. For whatever reason, you just agree. Perhaps you surrender to the higher authority. Perhaps you are just trying to make friends. You just want people to like you. In most cases, you just don't care that much about the subject matter of the conflict.

When we *avoid* (Q2), we refuse to participate in any effort to discuss or address the conflict. We look the other way. We harbor ill feelings about the conflict but choose not to do anything about it. We are hostile to the other party and this often devolves into passive-aggressive behavior.

When we *compromise*, we split the difference. Neither party gets what they really want or need. What you get and what I get adds up to 100 percent of what we imagine as the solution. Maybe we split it 50-50. Or maybe it's 80-20. But we fail to find a way that both parties can succeed more fully. We fail to collaborate.

Each of these first four approaches has a fatal flaw. To compete is to have disregard for the relationship with the other person. To accommodate is to have low concern for the task. To avoid shows little or no regard for either the task at hand or the relationship with the other person. To compromise is to fail to imagine the possibilities of collaboration.

It is important to distinguish *conflict avoidance* from *conflict prevention*. Preventing a conflict from escalating from task conflict to relational conflict is a good thing. Avoiding the conflict once it has already been launched can be destructive to both the task at hand and the relationships involved. It can escalate a conflict into relationship conflict.

YOUR CONFLICT APPROACH IS SITUATIONAL.

Nevertheless, Thomas says there are certain *situations* when you might want to compete, accommodate, avoid, or compromise—but only in rare occasions. For example, when the other party is very aggressive, and the environment is competitive, you might need to become more competitive to meet their force. When the task is not a priority of yours, and others feel passionate about it, you might want to be more agreeable. When tempers flare, it might be appropriate to avoid the conflict, but only temporarily, until cooler heads prevail. When time is of the essence, compromise might be the best solution.

The optimal approach to conflict is *collaboration* (Q4). As the model shows, this approach is highest in concern for both the task and the relationship. To be collaborative means you are *assertive* about the task and *cooperative* on the relationship—at the same time! Not easy to do. This is Q4 behavior. We will address this later in the Three-Step Meeting.

Note: When we teach this model, we usually suggest that there is space within the Q4 quadrant and that we might move in the direction of Q1 or Q3—without crossing over the line into that quadrant. For example, you might be at the Christmas party when someone initiates a discussion about some conflict brewing in the parish. It might be appropriate at that time to move toward a less assertive approach (Q3) but to make it clear that the conflict will be addressed at another time.

Reflection Questions

- When you move out of the collaborative approach to conflict, are you more likely to compete, avoid, or accommodate?
- What situational factors are most likely to move you to compete, avoid, or accommodate?

Conflict Model

Conflict begins when I become aware that you have done something, or plan to do something, that jeopardizes something that I care about (Thomas). Immediately, I have *thoughts* and *emotions* that flood my brain. My thoughts affect my emotions and vice versa.

Based on my reaction, I develop *intentions* about how I will respond. My intentions are not always consistent with my actions. They are simply what I intend to do. Following the five styles just described, my intentions are either (Q1) compete, (Q2) avoid, (Q3) accommodate, (Q4) collaborate, or compromise.

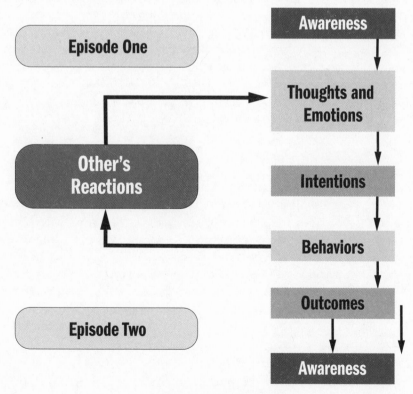

The Thomas Model of Conflict

Then I act. My *action* stirs thoughts, emotions, and intentions on the part of the other person—let's say that it is *you*. Your perception of my action might be totally different from my intention. Perhaps I had intended to collaborate, but you perceived my action as an attack.

Then *you* react to my action. Your *reaction* stirs another round of thoughts, emotions, and intentions on my part. My perception of your action may be totally different from your intention. Perhaps you intended to collaborate, but I perceived your actions as an attack.

And I react. And so on. This can go on for days, weeks, months, even years.

EMOTIONS MOVE US INTO ACTION.

Let's say that you are in a parish meeting when someone says something that upsets you. Unless you pay thoughtful attention to what is happening, your emotions will immediately distort your view of reality. They will cloud your judgment and affect everything you say and do. Before reacting, it is important to find that place of calm where you can change your perspective.

Remember that the first place our senses report to the brain stem is the limbic area controlled by emotions. Any neurological sensation must travel through the emotional region of the brain before entering the cognitive and judgment parts of the brain.

EMOTIONAL DISTRESS REDUCES MENTAL CLARITY.

Emotions can overwhelm the connecting points of our brains to the point where we cannot think straight. For example, if you are prone to worry, then worrying will overwhelm the circuitry in your brain. Worrying is a cognitive task that breaks down our ability to concentrate on other tasks. Therefore, our worries can become a self-fulfilling prophecy. Our performance suffers when we worry.

Being quick to judge, quick to anger, slow to adapt, and slow to understand—these are signs of emotional distress. *Temperance* is the virtue associated with controlling our *temper* or handling our emotional distress. Temperance does not shut emotions out of brain activity. It gives emotions a balanced role that is proportionate to the situation. As Daniel Goleman points out, emotions have a way of disturbing the brain's activity of processing information.

NOT ALL IDEAS LEAD TO ACTION, BUT MOST EMOTIONS DO.

When I am edgy, nervous, or irritable, my physiological reaction to a situation is likely to interpret your behavior as a hostile attack, thus triggering more adrenaline and escalating my hormonal momentum.

When we feel emotional distress, especially when our emotions boil over, the tendency is to move quickly into action. Our thoughts and emotions get mixed together. In a heated environment, emotions tend to take over. Emotions can move us into autopilot. We lose perspective. We act without reason.

When any negative experience presents itself to us, we quickly and reflexively shift the focus of our brain activity to the most primitive of instincts, our hindbrain, the amygdala. This is a limbic reflex that is difficult to control. The amygdala signals to us to be more self-centered, only concerned for our own basic survival and protection.

Remember, when we get angry, the brain sends energy to the hands—preparing us to hit something or someone. When we are afraid, the brain sends energy to the feet—preparing us to flee. Thus, we tread between fight (anger) or flight (fear). This translates into either compete (Q1) or avoid (Q2), which explains why those two responses to conflict are so common.

Action that emits from the prefrontal cortex takes more time because more brain circuitry is involved. Remember that research with the Dalai Lama's yogis shows that their minds can quickly shift attention toward the prefrontal cortex, within milliseconds (Begley). For most of us, however, it takes about six seconds for brain activity to involve the prefrontal cortex.

Research shows that emotions are less powerful once they are named (Goleman). Naming emotions lowers the traumatic impact on the body. Perhaps this is because naming the emotion triggers self-awareness.

Reflective probes are statements that name the emotion you are noticing in the other person, for example, "You seem frustrated, what can I do to help?" Or "If that happened to me, I know that I would be upset." Let's say the other person is angry. Their brain is releasing a chemical response that increases their heart rate. They can feel the anger in their gut. Research shows that just by acknowledging the anger that is present, we reduce the chemical response. The other person will become less angry when you name the emotion (Goleman).

A reflective probe helps the other person become aware of their emotional distress. It reveals to the other person that their emotional reaction has become apparent to someone else. The result: In many cases, the chemical reaction weakens in that other person. They become more self-aware. They are more likely to settle into a more objective view of reality.

During conflict, we cannot underestimate the importance of self-awareness for both parties. When we pause, reflect, and become self-aware before making decisions and taking action, the prefrontal lobes are playing a greater role in our decision-making process. From there, we can connect to the heart. We can feel some empathy. We can harmonize head and heart. When we are more conscious of the effect that emotions have on our actions and decisions, we become happier and healthier human beings.

One person can face a very stressful situation, and it might become their downfall. Another person can face a very similar stressful situation, and they might grow in wisdom. The difference? Often, it is taking time to pray and reflect on that experience.

WISDOM IS KNOWLEDGE BASED ON EXPERIENCE PLUS REFLECTION.

Perception becomes our reality. For example, if you perceive that I am being rude, then I am. At the end of the day, it doesn't matter what my intentions were. It is your perception of my action that counts. If you think I am being rude, then I am being rude. My job is to deal with your perceptions. This requires an ability to pick up on the emotions of the other person.

To be human is to be emotional. To feel negative emotions like fear, anger, frustration, or jealousy is normal. The challenge is to do something constructive with that emotion. Figure out how to learn and grow from the experience. Identify the emotion. Approach it directly. Ask yourself: *Why am I afraid? How do I become angry? What makes me frustrated? Why am I jealous?* This takes prayerful, mindful reflection.

Three-Step Meeting

When you are engaged in conflict, try this three-step meeting to resolve, contain, or navigate the conflict.

First, listen to the other person. Find out what the conflict looks like from their perspective. As St. Francis suggested, "Seek first to understand, then to be understood." In a conflict situation, it is always better to let the other person explain their perspective first. People are generally more interested in what you have to say once you have shown interest in what they have to say.

Listen attentively. Listen from your heart. Not from your amygdala. If the other person is criticizing something that you have done, think it through carefully, using more reason and less emotion. Be reflective of their emotions and yours. Separate the other person from their criticism of your action (Fisher and Ury). Realize that describing a failed event is not saying that you are a failure. Weigh ideas truthfully and perspectives objectively.

Active, reflective, and responsive listening will increase their receptivity to listen to you. As they present their story, summarize their ideas, reflect their emotions, and ask, "Did I get that right?" "Is there anything else?" "How do you want me to help?" Once you have carefully listened to their story—and demonstrated this with reflective probes and accurate summaries—they are much more likely to listen to your story.

Second, explain your perspective. Be assertive about your needs. Be clear about your interests. Remember that collaboration requires that you are both assertive and cooperative at the same time. Speak from the heart. Try not to blame, exaggerate, or do anything that will incite emotional distress on their part.

Take some of the blame for the conflict. Acknowledge your mistakes. View them as lessons for the future. Recognize that mistakes today can make us better tomorrow. To be human is to make mistakes. Accepting blame makes you easier to work with.

---

1. LISTEN.   2. EXPLAIN.   3. MERGE.

Compliment the other person for something they said. Find some area of agreement with what they have shared. Point out that you both are committed to the mission of the parish. Appeal to their higher instincts and you will help bring out the best version of that person. Take the high road.

Third, merge perspectives. Search for a common understanding of the conflict. My colleague Randy Richards suggests that one way to accomplish this is by articulating a *neutral statement of the conflict*. This is a less adversarial and more collegial statement of what both parties agree is the essence of the conflict. Begin with, "The issue between us is…" or "Here is the problem we face together…."

Try to focus the conversation on solutions that meet the concerns of both parties. Take on the other person's interest as if it is your own. Ask the other person the following:

Can you think of any ideas that might solve the problem for both of us?

What would it take for the two of us to get beyond this impasse?

If we had this to do all over again, how would we do things differently?

Solving the conflict in a way that benefits both parties will only serve to strengthen the relationship for the future.

Reflection Questions

- What is a recent conflict you experienced?
- Try to write a neutral statement of that conflict.

Three Pathways for Step Three

My colleague Randy Richards suggests that what path you take to resolve the conflict in step three (above) will depend on which of three types of conflict you are experiencing.

An *interest conflict* occurs when you have opposing interests. It might be two parties warring over scarce resources. In an interest conflict, you can often find common ground where both parties collaborate to get what they want or need. You look for what Fisher and Ury call "options for mutual gain."

A *factual conflict* happens when you have two different versions of what happened, or a disagreement about the facts in the case. It might be two different interpretations of a policy, procedure, or practice. In a factual conflict, you can often reach agreement by finding an expert source, or someone who is an expert, or an accepted policy that relates to the conflict. You look for what Fisher and Ury call "objective criteria."

A *normative conflict* materializes when your values and beliefs are in conflict. It might be a difference of opinion about policies such as dress code, practices such as tardiness, traditions such as the American flag, priorities such as strategies, values such as safety, or behaviors such as whether someone else *should* be allowed to do something. In normative conflicts, resolution is complicated. These conflicts require more dialogue to come to a better appreciation for what each party values and why they behave as they do. Ask yourself the following questions:

- What was the context of the other person's behavior?
- What choices did the other person have in that situation?
- Why did they choose to do what they did?
- What do you think would have been a better choice?
- Why do you think that is preferable?
- What should we do differently in the future?

Remember that dialogue about any conflict cannot seem like a lecture. It is a conversation. Dialogue begins with an authentic desire to learn and grow from the conflict.

This will take some time. Leading change—especially when conflict is involved—may not happen in *chronos* time. It may take *kairos* time. In *chronos* time, we often think, "I don't have time for this." In *kairos* time, we allow the change process to proceed with faith in God, with trust in each other, and with confidence in the process itself.

Patience

It takes *patience* to orchestrate, resolve, and navigate our way through conflict and to allow people to be involved in choosing the change they want to see. One of the fruits of the Holy Spirit (Gal 5:22), patience has been described by Pope Francis as the "mother of mercy."

LET US RUN THE RACE BEFORE US WITH PATIENCE (HEB 12:1).

Tertullian said that patience is "God's nature." Lactantius called it the "greatest of virtues." Virtues like patience are learned through developing habits and creating dispositions that shape our character.

As we act with virtues, we retrain our minds and reform our hearts for the difficult challenges of leadership (1 Pet 1:5–7).

Chapter Summary

In this chapter, we reflected on how to lead *adaptive change* by getting on the balcony, thinking politically, and orchestrating the conflict. Leadership challenges are plentiful. Leaders to address those challenges are not so plentiful. Leading change involves stimulating healthy conflict without letting it escalate into relationship conflict.

The next chapter looks at how pastoral leaders can involve the entire parish as they address their leadership challenges. We will consider the idea of *strategic pastoral planning*, which takes our eight steps of strategic planning and incorporates it into the parish process called pastoral planning. We will discuss the roles of mission, vision, and core values.

References

Allison, Michael, and Jude Kaye. *Strategic Planning for Nonprofit Organizations: A Practical Guide and Workbook*. New York: Support Center for Non-Profit Management, John Wiley and Sons, 2005.

Begley, Sharon. *Train Your Mind, Change Your Brain: How a New Science Reveals Our Extraordinary Potential to Transform Ourselves*. New York: Ballantine Books, 2007.

Bryson, John M. *Strategic Planning for Public and Nonprofit Organizations: A Guide to Strengthening and Sustaining Organizational Achievement*. 3rd ed. San Francisco: Jossey-Bass, 2004.

Cloke, Kenneth, and Joan Goldsmith. *Resolving Conflict at Work: A Complete Guide for Everyone on the Job*. San Francisco: Jossey-Bass, 2010.

Fisher, Roger, and William Ury. *Getting to Yes: Negotiating Agreement without Giving In*. New York: Penguin Books, 1981.

French, John R., and Bertram Raven. "The Bases of Social Power." In *Studies in Social Power*, edited by D. Cartwright. Ann Arbor, MI: Institute for Social Research, 1959.

Goleman, Daniel. *Emotional Intelligence*. New York: Bantam Dell, 2005.

Greenleaf, Robert K. *The Servant Leader Within: The Transformative Path*. Edited by Hamilton Beazley, Julie Beggs, and Larry C. Spears. Mahwah, NJ: Paulist Press, 2003.

Ebener, Dan R. *Servant Leadership Models for Your Parish*. Mahwah, NJ: Paulist Press, 2010.

Ebener, Dan R., and Frederick L. Smith. *Strategic Planning: An Interactive Process for Leaders*. Mahwah, NJ: Paulist Press, 2015.

Heifetz, Ronald A. *Leadership without Easy Answers*. Boston: Harvard Business School Press, 1994.

Heifetz, Ronald A., and Marty Linsky. *Leadership on the Line: Staying Alive through the Dangers of Leading*. Boston: Harvard Business School Press, 2002.

Heifetz, Ronald A., Alexander Grashow, and Marty Linsky. *The Practice of Adaptive Leadership: Tools and Tactics for Changing Your Organizations and the World*. Boston: Harvard Business School Press, 2009.

Isaacs, William. *Dialogue and the Art of Thinking Together: A Pioneering Approach to Communicating in Business and in Life*. New York: Doubleday, 1999.

Jehn, Karen A. "A Multimethod Examination of the Benefits and Detriments of Intragroup Conflict." *Administrative Science Quarterly* 40 (1995): 256–82.

Jehn, Karen A., and Elizabeth A. Mannix. "The Dynamic Nature of Conflict: A Longitudinal Study of Intragroup Conflict and Group Performance." *Academy of Management Journal* 44 (2001): 238–51.

Kotter, John P. *Leading Change*. Boston: Harvard Business School Press, 1996.

Marquardt, Michael J. *Leading with Questions: How Leaders Find the Right Solutions by Knowing What to Ask*. San Francisco: Jossey-Bass, 2014.

Olson, Edwin E., and Glenda H. Eoyang. *Facilitating Organization Change: Lessons from Complexity Science*. San Francisco: Jossey-Bass, 2001.

Pope Francis, from "A Big Heart Open to God." *America*, September 19, 2013.

Richards, Randy L. *Conflict and Collaboration: The Search for the Integrative Space.* Rock Island, IL: Randy Richards, 2017.

Rost, Joseph C. *Leadership for the Twenty-First Century.* New York: Praeger Publishers, 1991.

Scharmer, Otto, and Katrin Kaufer. *Leading from the Emerging Future: From Ego-System to Eco-System Economies: Applying Theory U to Transforming Business, Society, and Self.* San Francisco: Berrett-Koehler Publishers, 2013.

Schein, Edgar H. *Humble Inquiry: The Gentle Art of Asking Instead of Telling.* San Francisco: Berrett-Koehler, 2013.

Thomas, Kenneth W. "Conflict and Negotiation Processes in Organizations." In *Handbook of Industrial and Organizational Psychology,* edited by Marvin D. Dunnette and Leaetta M. Hough. Vol. 3, 2nd ed. Palo Alto, CA: Consulting Psychologist Press, 1992.

Williams, Dean. *Real Leadership: Helping People and Organizations Face Their Toughest Challenges.* San Francisco: Berrett-Koehler Publishers, 2005.

Chapter 5

Strategic Pastoral Planning

Chapter 5 Preview

In this chapter, we will consider the following:

- How *pastoral planning* is similar but different from *strategic planning*
- A new concept we will call *strategic pastoral planning*
- How to facilitate the eight steps of strategic pastoral planning
- How *mission* is the bottom line and *vision* is the picture of success
- The role of leaders and managers in the planning process
- How to *plan the work* so that you *work the plan*

St. Michael's—The Challenge of Planning

Fr. Dave was now aware of the adaptive challenges he faced at St. Michael's. He realized that the parish needed to address these challenges. It was tempting to just sit down and articulate his own vision and write a strategic plan to guide the parish into action. After all, he had a good idea about what the parish needed.

He also realized that such a plan would be *his* plan only. It would lack ownership by anyone else. Therefore, it was unlikely to go anywhere. The laypeople would not be excited about implementing a plan they were not involved in creating. He needed a way to bring the parish together and get everyone on the same page about a manageable number of priorities.

In this chapter, we will see how Fr. Dave can involve his parish council, staff, and lay leaders in a strategic planning process that works well in parishes. It is a process that Fred Smith and I wrote up in a book entitled *Strategic Planning: An Interactive Process for Leaders*.

A Parish Plans

It was the night before the big event. Fr. Dave was expecting 175 parishioners to show up to participate in a pastoral planning session. As he visited with friends that evening, Fr. Dave reflected, "My brother priests think I'm crazy. They think I have invited 175 people to tell me how to do my job! Besides, isn't the pastor supposed to have the vision?"

Indeed, 175 people did show up the next day. They were lively and energetic throughout the five hours of planning. They began with prayer and reflection on parish mission, using the parable of the sower and the seed. Parishioners discussed the sower as the evangelist, the seed as the Word of God, and the soil as the heart of the person receiving the Word. They discussed how planning offered them a new opportunity to till the soil of the parish and sow the seed into the hearts of their community.

The parish council president presented some data from the *CARA Report* about trends in the Church on (1) Vocations, (2) Migration, (3) Immigration, (4) Formation, and (5) Participation. After discussing these and other trends in the Church, parishioners shared insights into their own Strengths and Weaknesses. They also shared stories about how changes in the Church and the world were presenting the parish with Opportunities and Threats.

With people sitting at thirty-six tables, they had nine sets of *conversation cafes* (with four tables per set). It took a lot of facilitation that will be explained in this chapter. The result was nine charts full of information describing the Strengths, Weaknesses, Opportunities, and Threats (SWOT) of the parish. To bring it all together, they did a *gallery walk*, which meant posting all the information generated at the thirty-six tables, and asking people to walk around the room, studying the results of their SWOT, looking for common themes and visiting with each other.

Then they went back and discussed the most important decision in planning:

What are our strategic issues?

After considerable facilitation, three themes emerged from their thirty-six small-group conversations: (1) Engagement, (2) Evangelization, and (3) Ministry to youth and young adults. These strategic issues were articulated as three *strategic questions*:

1. ***How can we*** engage more parishioners to become more actively involved in the parish and more willing to lead parish initiatives?

2. ***How can we*** reach out to those outside our parish community with evangelization and outreach?

3. ***How can we*** encourage youth, young adults, and young families to get more involved in practicing the Catholic faith?

After lunch, the parishioners took those three strategic questions and dove into discussions about what they could do to respond. Possible answers to the strategic questions became *strategies*. When they deleted the *How Can We* part of each strategic question, they had their three strategic goals. What follows are their three strategic goals, each with three to four strategies:

1. Improve Lay Engagement	1.1 To form small faith communities
	1.2 To create a culture of personal invitation
	1.3 To develop and foster leadership
	1.4 To go deeper into our spirituality
2. Enhance Evangelization and Outreach	2.1 To sponsor fun community events
	2.2 To assign a "buddy" or "buddy family" to new or inactive members
	2.3 To market the parish
3. Involve Youth and Young Adults	3.1 To formally establish a young adult (18–39) ministry
	3.2 To hold targeted social events and service projects for youth and young adults
	3.3 To optimize use of social media

Before adjourning, everyone was invited to spend one more hour working in a small group focused on one of the ten strategies (above). Their job was to develop specific action items, with timelines and names of people responsible for each item (below). That way, the parish council could start with very specific ways to work on the three strategic goals and ten strategies. People volunteered to help with each of the action steps. With 175 parishioners present, this afforded lots of opportunities for new leaders to emerge!

Examples of some of the action steps included the following:

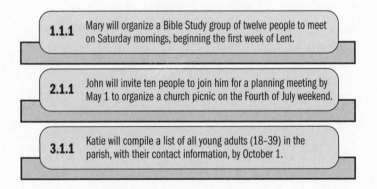

1.1.1 Mary will organize a Bible Study group of twelve people to meet on Saturday mornings, beginning the first week of Lent.

2.1.1 John will invite ten people to join him for a planning meeting by May 1 to organize a church picnic on the Fourth of July weekend.

3.1.1 Katie will compile a list of all young adults (18–39) in the parish, with their contact information, by October 1.

At the end of the day, Fr. Dave was thrilled. Yes, he could have sat down and written up a similar plan for the parish in less than five hours. But then it would have been "Father's Plan." He could have persuaded the people to follow his vision. But that would have been a *charismatic* vision, not a *shared* vision.

This process provides insights from a wide variety of perspectives. The wide participation builds plenty of *buy-in* from the parish. It creates *enthusiasm* for ministry. People leave feeling excited about the future and clearer about the vision of the parish.

The process of setting goals says more about *what you can become* than what you can accomplish. It produces the joy that comes from reaching for your full potential.

Strategic Planning

Strategic planning is an interactive process where leaders, followers, and managers create a shared vision that includes strategic goals, strategies, and action steps.

The old metaphor for strategic planning was a *mountain-top retreat*. The most important people in the organization would spend several days planning for the next five to ten years. They would come down from the mountain, like Moses with the Ten Commandments, and present the plan to the people.

Today's metaphor is *whitewater rafting*. We are all in the same boat together, moving swiftly down that mountain, steering our way through raging waters. Change is swirling around us. We rely on each other at every twist and turn amidst the rocks. We trust each other to make quick decisions based on clear values, simple rules, and specific action steps.

The *furious* pace of change in today's world is not a good fit for the *glacial* pace of change within the Church. As a Church, we need to adapt to the new reality of a world that comes at us like a freight train.

Planning can and should be fun. It can be an opportunity for relationship building. Getting everyone on the same page helps build your team. Talking about mission and core values inspires people. Seeing change begin to happen builds a sense of hope and optimism. I've heard many parishioners say to me at the end of a day of planning, "I've been through some very painful strategic planning before...but this was fun...and we got a lot done."

Strategic Pastoral Planning

The main difference between strategic planning and pastoral planning is the discernment of the Holy Spirit. Pastoral planning asks,

To what is God calling us?

Pastoral planning is a time for a community of faith to remember why we exist. Opening each session with prayer and reflection on Scripture can be the most important aspect of planning. It reminds us of *who we are* and *who God is*. It brings us back to our mission of bringing Christ to others. It reminds us of Jesus' vision of the reign of God.

When we pray, "Thy kingdom come, thy will be done," we are reminded that building the kingdom is the vision of Jesus and the will of God. In pastoral planning, we discern what exactly that looks like in our parish.

HOW CAN WE BUILD THE KINGDOM?

We will always be a Church that first needs to pray and reflect. Prayer is at the core of our being. Sometimes we pray in our own words and sometimes we pray in the beautiful words of a prayer we have learned. But we pray. My mother taught me that the key to a balanced life is *to pray like everything is in God's hands and to work like everything is in our hands*.

The paradox of pastoral planning is this: How can we continuously adapt to the external change in a world moving so quickly, without sacrificing the need for prayer and reflection amidst the chaos?

How can we "keep alert" (1 Pet 5:8) to the constant changes in our world and "pray without ceasing" (1 Thess 5:17)?

Steps in Strategic Pastoral Planning

Pastoral planning is a time for the parish community to come together to plan strategically while discerning God's will for the parish. The paradox of God's will is that we are granted free will, only to discover the beauty of surrendering to God's will. It is by living the will of God that we can find true purpose and meaning in our lives.

Pastoral planning is a process of using our God-given free will to *discern the will of God*. We become servants to the plan that God has for us. We remain open to the movement of the Holy Spirit. We start with prayer and reflection. We listen and speak from our hearts. We get out of our comfort zone. We become forward thinking. We take risks.

WE ALIGN OUR WILL WITH GOD'S WILL.

Many people describe this as thinking *outside the box*. The box is depicted in the chart below as the "Strategy." It represents our "usual way of doing things around here," the old strategies that we resort to whenever we face a new challenge. *Inside the box* means the same people doing the same things. To get outside the box, we must dismiss the notion that "we tried that before and it doesn't work."

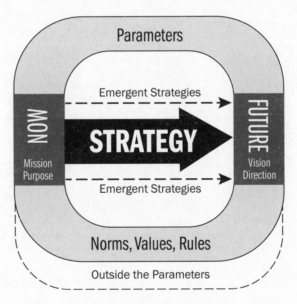

Outside the Box, Inside the Circle

As we think outside the box, we also need to think *inside the circle*. The circle represents the limits to which we can think outside the box. The limits in a Catholic parish includes Church law, scriptural values, or outside mandates, such as diocesan policies. Every organization has a limit to how far outside the box they can think. But there is usually plenty of space *outside the box but inside the circle* that has not yet been explored.

For example, canon law does not allow a Catholic parish to change the rules governing ordination. This may be very discouraging for some parishioners. They might think that canon law is shutting down opportunities for leadership. But if we define leadership as an activity that can be practiced outside of authority, then we don't need to be ordained to lead. We can *lead without ordination*. That is the space outside the box but inside the circle.

Many adaptive challenges require ***outside-the-box-but-inside-the-circle*** thinking. There is a need for and room for leadership from many directions. We need to set aside our mistakes of the past and open our minds and hearts to future ways of thinking and acting. In the fast-paced world we live in today, it is impossible for those in authority to have all the answers. It is naïve to expect that. We need to also tap into the *collective* experience of the group.

Next, I will apply our eight-step, *strategic planning* process to the needs for *pastoral planning*. We will call this a ***strategic pastoral planning process***. The core values for this process are (1) a focus on mission and values, (2) participation by as many stakeholders as possible, (3) interaction between the participants, (4) creation of a shared vision, and (5) continuous updates during implementation.

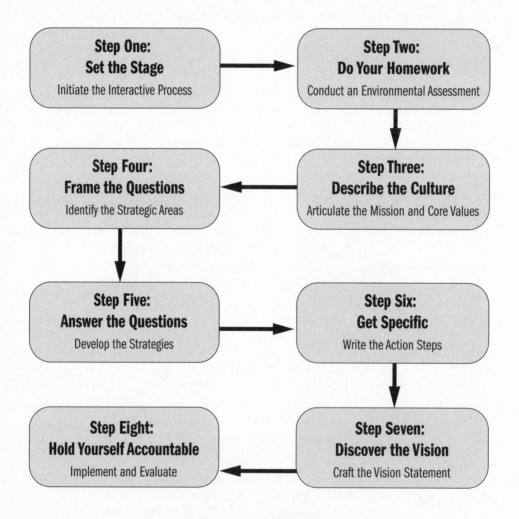

Our Strategic Planning Model

What follows are my suggested eight steps for *strategic pastoral planning*.

1. Plan the Plan

Before you can *work the plan*, you must *plan the work*. The first step is to *plan the plan*. The most important consideration is how you can involve as many members of the congregation as possible. More involvement gains two things:

> **First,** it gathers a wider range of ideas. If we all see a problem the same way, we are probably missing something. If we all come up with the same solution, we have *groupthink*. If we all look at a chandelier on the ceiling of a room, each of us sees the chandelier from one perspective. No one sees the entire chandelier. If we want to know what the other side of the chandelier looks like, we need to ask people who see it from a different angle of the room. In the same way, we need to involve people from all corners of the parish if we want to get the full view of what is happening.

> **Second,** more involvement creates more enthusiasm for the plan. When we are trying to get "buy-in," it means we are trying to sell something. Whatever plan emerges out of our pastoral planning, someone will need to sell it. Sure, the pastor and a few key people could write the strategic plan by themselves. It would be much easier. But then it would be the plan only of a few people. Selling the plan is much easier when people have participated in creating the plan.

THE FIRST STEP IS TO PLAN THE WORK.

SO LATER YOU CAN WORK THE PLAN.

One of the ways that you can involve some of the uninvolved, the less involved, or even the fallen away members of your parish is through focus groups. Invite people in any of these categories to an evening meal or a weekday luncheon with a focus group interview (see Appendix A).

Invite active parishioners to join a focus group session after each Mass. Gather their suggested strategies and ideas for improvement. Go to the meetings of each of the commissions and interview people to gain their perspective and ideas. Have someone take careful notes of all the input. Then share the reports with those attending the main sessions where the plan will be put together.

In most cases, the *pastoral planning team* (those creating the plan) for a parish would be the clergy, staff, lay trustees, parish council, and finance council of the parish. Chairpersons of each commission would also be invited.

However, it is possible to hold interactive planning sessions with up to hundreds of people. (See *Strategic Planning: An Interactive Process for Leaders* for more ideas on just how to set up and facilitate such meetings.)

The other logistical issues involved with planning to plan include *where* and *when* to hold the planning sessions, *who* will facilitate, *how long* the sessions will go, and *which* of the following steps to include in the process. Generally, we recommend two three-hour planning sessions scheduled about two to six weeks apart. But it depends on many factors we will consider next.

2. Do Your Homework

To assess your environment: First, look *within* your parish and ask what is going well (your strengths), what could be better (your weaknesses), and how could you improve on those weaknesses. Second,

---

look *outside* your parish and ask what changes in the world are creating opportunities for growth, challenges to that growth (threats), and how you could adapt to those changes.

Together, this input helps you conduct a SWOT analysis, where you identify internal Strengths (S) and Weaknesses (W) and external Opportunities (O) and Threats (T). Think of strengths and weaknesses as being those factors *within* your control. Think of opportunities as trends in the Church or society that are working in our favor. Threats are trends in the Church or society working against our efforts. Opportunities and threats are *outside* your control.

LOOK FOR FACTORS INSIDE AND OUTSIDE YOUR CONTROL.

One way that parishes can do the internal part of their homework is to ask their own people for ideas and suggestions for improvement. This can be done through focus groups, interviews, or surveys. Involving people who are not very involved in the parish helps us to identify our blind spots, the things we don't see because we are too close to it.

Strengths can be weaknesses and vice versa. Facilities, liturgy, music, finances, outreach, and virtually every aspect of being church can wind up on both sides of the ledger. For example, music might be a strength because we love our choir. It might also be a weakness because very few people are singing with the choir. Full, active, and conscious participation in the liturgy requires involvement.

Identifying the opportunities and threats can be trickier. Once again, threats can be opportunities and vice versa. For example, cell phones can be a useful opportunity for improved communication, but they become a threat when they are going off during a meeting. With every threat, every obstacle, every crisis, and every challenge, comes an opportunity for change.

Conduct an environmental assessment of the current trends in the Church. The book, *Catholic Parishes of the 21st Century*, outlines data on many trends, including (1) Vocations, (2) Migration, (3) Immigration, (4) Formation, and (5) Participation (Zech et al.).

Let's look at vocations as an example. While priestly vocations have decreased by 26 percent (from 34,000 to 25,000) over the past generation (from 1990 to 2015), the number of Catholic Church employees over that same period has *increased by 20 percent* (from 55,000 to 64,000) (Zech et al.). This means fewer priests but more laypeople working for the Church, which is similar to the early Church.

We usually only hear about the shortage of priests. However, with more people working for the Church today, it stands to reason that we should expect more activity, more participation, and more leadership in the Church.

Another look at trends in the Church was the *Emerging Models of Leadership* study funded by the Lilly Endowment. It concluded with three lessons that should inform Catholic planners: (1) people in parishes learn best in small groups; (2) people are longing for the connectedness they can find in Sunday liturgy; and (3) people want to protect the Catholic traditions of the Church (Ganim).

The Pew Research Center informs us that the percentage of the U.S. population that is Catholic has been in decline. The Catholic population is propped up somewhat by the growth in Latino Catholics. But overall, the percent of the U.S. population that is Catholic has gone down from 23.9 percent in 2007 to 20.8 percent in 2014.

In fact, Albert Winseman of Gallup reports that organized religion has been "in serious decline" for almost fifty years. Congregational membership has been decreasing despite the fact that church members are "more than three times as likely as nonmembers to be fully spiritually committed" (Winseman).

FACE YOUR CURRENT REALITY WITH OPEN EYES.

The group that is growing fastest are those who do not identify with any religion. They are called the *Nones*. They have been on the rise since the 1980s. Pew says that 22.8 percent of Americans are Nones (note that this is higher than the Catholic population). Among young adults (under thirty years of age), 33 percent are Nones. The Nones may believe in God. They might even pray, but they do not associate with any religion.

Another growing segment, and now the largest religious group in the United States, are the Evangelical Protestants, now at 25.4 percent of the U.S. population (Pew, 2014). White mainline Protestants make up only 14.7 percent. Black Protestant churches are at 6.5 percent. Altogether, Protestants are now only 46.6 percent of the population.

The ethnic makeup of U.S. Catholics has also shifted in the past generation. Among Catholics, only 55 percent are white Catholic (a number that was 87 percent in 1981) and 36 percent are Hispanic. Among young adult Catholics (under the age of thirty), 52 percent are Hispanic and only 36 percent are white (Cox and Jones).

These numbers indicate a new reality for all parishes. The issues, challenges, and problems *out there* are *in here*, too. These trends have many implications for pastoral planning. Creating the future starts with learning from the past and facing the reality of the present.

Discussion Question
What are the most influential trends in the Church today?

For example: What can we learn from the increase in the Nones? Perhaps we should organize a team of parish visitors to go out and conduct interviews with the Nones in our neighborhoods. Find out what their needs and interests are. What can we learn about the growth of Evangelical Protestants? Perhaps we need to visit their churches to see what we can learn. This would certainly get us out of our comfort zone.

3. Reflect on Mission and Core Values

The mission of God has a Church. That Church needs to be clear about that mission as it moves into pastoral planning. In fact, the mission and core values ought to drive all strategic decision-making.

MISSION IS ABOUT PURPOSE.

The core of mission is *purpose*. Ask yourselves the following: *What is our reason for being? Why do we exist? What is our nobler cause? What benefit do we contribute to the common good?*

The second part of a mission statement is called your *business*. Ask yourselves these questions: *What do we do? What activities are at the core of our identity?*

After some small and large group discussion about mission and core values, write a mission statement that is both memorable and memorizable. Once you create your mission statement, find ways to get it out there: on your website, at the bottom of financial reports, at the bottom of meeting agendas, on the back of business cards, in the bulletin, and on the bulletin board.

At Immaculate Conception Parish in Florence, Wisconsin, they state together their mission statement as part of their weekly announcements at the end of each Mass. The lector proclaims the first half of the mission statement, "To live the gospel," and the congregation responds, "Whatever it takes."

Pastoral planning is a time to stretch our minds about ways to accomplish our mission. That means stretching our dollars as well. As a parish does more mission, it will be easier to raise more money. Remember that the Notre Dame research shows that people give more generously to mission than they do to needs (Starks and Smith). Every mission has a margin, and every wallet has a will. Appeal to mission and you will raise the money.

4. Identify Strategic Issues

Once the homework is done, and the environmental assessment is concluded, the pastoral planning team faces their most critical decision: Identifying the *strategic issues*. These are the most significant challenges facing your parish. They get articulated first as questions starting with "How can we...," and eventually they are reworded as your strategic goals.

Strategic issues can be identified by studying the environmental assessment. Ask yourself the following: *What are the greatest changes occurring in our world?* and *How do our strengths and weaknesses line up with our opportunities and threats?* For example:

- *What strengths can we leverage to take advantage of our opportunities?*
- *What strengths will help us protect against our threats?*
- *What weaknesses need to be strengthened so we can act on our opportunities?*
- *What weaknesses need to be strengthened to protect against our threats?*

Let's say that you have been tracking the calls into your parish to determine the *on-ramping* activity. You see a pattern and recognize it as an opportunity for evangelization.

Let's also say that a weakness in your parish is that the core leaders are exhausted. The same people show up to do the same things. You need new energy. Therefore, the strategic issue might be this:

How can we *develop new leaders for the ministry of evangelization?*

Strategic issues are *important* but not necessarily perceived as *urgent*. For example, developing new leaders may be something that the parish has needed for years. It is important, but perhaps no one has created a sense of urgency about it (Kotter). Strategic pastoral planning demands that we become more strategic about our time and resources. It is time to refocus on the most important matters we are not addressing.

The key is to eliminate some of the things we are doing that are *urgent but not important*, so we can make time for those things that are *important but not urgent*. Our most difficult issues will not go away without refocusing our time and attention toward them. They demand new energy. They are screaming for someone to step up to practice leadership.

Some Examples of Strategic Issues

- **How can we** evangelize the unchurched in our neighborhood?
- **How can we** reach out to youth and young families?
- **How can we** become more gracious stewards of our gifts?
- **How can we** serve the poor while addressing the causes of poverty?
- **How can we** develop more active leadership for our ministries?
- **How can we** become more welcoming?

Discussion Question
What are the strategic issues facing your parish?

There are no easy answers here. These issues are fraught with adaptive challenges. Solutions are fleeting. Technical aspects might provide some consolation. However, if there was a technical solution to the above questions, we would have applied it by now. These strategic issues will require adaptive leadership.

Remember: ***Adaptive challenges require a change of hearts and minds.***

They require a change in people's attitudes and behaviors. This is precisely the work that Jesus calls for in his Sermon on the Mount (Matt 5—7). He calls us to change the way we think and act. He calls for a radical transformation of our hearts and minds (Rom 8).

The tendency is to resort to technical fixes precisely because they are easy, or because we want to avoid conflict. Sometimes, there may be technical aspects to a strategic issue, steps that can easily be taken to alleviate a problem. But we cannot stop with the technical fix.

For example, we might make our Church seem more welcoming by creating more attractive signage. We might even build a new church hall or redesign the sanctuary of the church itself. These are technical fixes that can help us be more welcoming. They require no change of heart. However, if the people continue to be *cold-hearted* toward newcomers and outsiders, the remodeled church will still feel cold and unwelcoming.

Unless you have a very large parish with plenty of untapped resources, it is best to limit your strategic issues to *three*. Later you will be adding strategies to each strategic issue. You will also be adding action steps to each strategy. Let's say you go with five strategic issues, five strategies per issue, and five action steps per strategy, you will end up with 125 new things to do!

The key is to be *parsimonious yet rigorous*. Make your plan realistic. Better to focus on about three strategic issues, with about three strategies per issue and three action steps per strategy. That multiplies to about twenty-seven new things to do!

Strategic goals cascade into strategies, which cascade into action steps, as depicted below.

5. Develop Strategies

Strategies are possible ways to answer the strategic questions listed earlier. Once we prioritize two or three strategic issues, the next step is to explore possible ways of addressing both the technical and adaptive aspects of the issue.

You can use conversation cafes to generate dialogue in a timely manner. Let's say that your strategic issues are (1) *How can we grow this parish?* (2) *How can we develop more active leaders?* and (3) *How can we engage our youth and young adults?* Divide the pastoral planning team into three groups, assigning each small group to a table that has a chart with one of your three strategic questions written at the top.

After about eight to ten minutes, rotate each group to the next table, one that has a different one of the three strategic questions. Each group (1) reads the comments on the chart as written by the first group, (2) highlights the ideas that are most helpful, and (3) adds their own written comments on the chart at their table.

After another eight to ten minutes, rotate each group to their third table. They (1) read the comments from the first two groups, (2) highlight the ideas that are most helpful, and (3) add their own written comments. In this way, each group builds on the ideas of the previous group(s).

FACILITATION TAKES YOUR FULL ATTENTION.

In this type of interaction, it is important to assign (1) a facilitator at each table to guide the interaction and (2) a scribe to write down the comments as they emerge. The scribe should write down the comments shared at that table without vetting every idea and waiting for everyone to agree on each item. Slowing down the process to reach consensus on each item limits the synergy that can be generated with rapid fire sharing of ideas.

After eight to ten minutes at the third chart, rotate each small group back to their original chart. Ask them to look at what has been added and what has been highlighted, then summarize all the information on the chart at their table into two to three overall themes. Tell them that these three themes will become strategies for that strategic issue. Test the whole team for consensus on the themes that emerge at each table.

Remember that strategic pastoral planning creates a safe space for risk-taking—*inside the circle but outside the box.* We all have our blind spots. Like junior partners in a law firm, or freshmen in a college, new members in a parish can see things the rest of us miss. Sharing those ideas will require trust, which can be built by practicing the active listening skills we discussed earlier.

Parish Activity

To brainstorm strategies, ask yourself the following:

- Given our strengths as a parish, and our current weaknesses, what suggestions for improvement can we give in this area of concern?

- Given the current opportunities and threats we are facing, and how they match up with our strengths and weaknesses, what strategies can we suggest?

6. Create an Action Plan

The *action plan* is what you will do in the first year of a pastoral plan. It answers the question of *who is going to do what by when?* The action plan sets the stage for later accountability and creates the support for future success.

Let's say you set a new year's resolution to spend more time each day in prayer. You are more likely to reach that goal if you tell someone. Sharing that information with others makes you more likely to hold yourself accountable to reach your goal and more likely to receive support from those who know about your goal.

ALIGN ACCOUNTABILITY WITH EACH RESPONSIBILITY.

For each strategy identified earlier, write out three to four *action steps*. These are very specific things you will do to act on that strategy. The key is to articulate each step with enough specificity that you know when and whether the action is done. This means using sentences with *finite* verbs and concrete actions like "Schedule an event," "Conduct a survey," "Place an ad," "Visit ten people," "Make ten phone calls," "Hold a meeting," "Consult with Jane Smith," "Recruit a new chairperson," or "Organize a training." By using specific, finite verbs like these, you will later be able to tell if these actions were taken. We call these "Go/No Go's" because at the end of the day, you can say whether the action was a "Go" or "No Go."

Each action step should have the name of a person who is going to be responsible and report on whether progress was made on that item. Each step needs a timeline. We suggest three, six, nine, or twelve months. Any action that needs more than one year needs to be further broken down into more immediate steps. Then you can hold *accountability sessions* once every three months to check in with each other, evaluate the pastoral plan, and update it with new action steps when needed.

This is what we call *working the plan*.

Remember that when you are driving down a road, the farther you look ahead, the less clear it gets. Action steps should be scheduled to be done in a timely manner. Once finished, they are archived and replaced with the next step(s) you will take when you update the plan.

WORK THE PLAN AND PLAN THE WORK.

7. Capture the Shared Vision

Many strategic planning models begin with stating a vision. My experience suggests that when it is done that way, the vision is usually articulated by a charismatic person in the group. This is not the same as a *shared vision*.

We are all cocreators in a shared vision.

Once you have completed steps one through six above, the vision question is this:

If we accomplish this strategic plan...if we live out our mission, address our strategic issues, pursue our strategies, and take these action steps, how is the world a better place?

Ask people to submit words or phrases that come to mind in answering this question. Assemble the responses. Ask two or three people to articulate a vision statement based on this input.

VISION IS ABOUT DIRECTION.

Like a mission statement, a vision statement should be memorable and memorizable. It should paint a picture of what future success would look like. My suggestion is to use an *external* vision statement, which focuses on how success would improve the world outside the parish. An *internal* vision statement focuses on how success would improve the parish.

A vision statement should be inspiring and energizing. Once adopted, place it in front of the people to remind them of our targeted result. Think of how often we reflect on the vision of Jesus. We share in it every time we pray, "Thy kingdom come, thy will be done on earth as it is in heaven." A parish vision statement should reflect some glimpse of the kingdom.

When conducted at the end of a strategic planning process, vision is discovered together instead of imposed upon by a few. The vision is created in the plan. Think of it as what Oliver Wendell Holmes called "simplicity on the other side of complexity," instead of simplicity without going through the complexity. Dialogue about vision is our last step in the final session of strategic pastoral planning.

Mission is about purpose. Vision focuses on direction. Vision changes as the world changes. Mission remains constant. More parishes struggle with vision than mission. They know their mission but do not know how to accomplish it. They have no plan. Without a plan, the vision fades.

Writing a vision statement, or a mission statement, should be delegated to a small group, with one person designated as the primary author. Wordsmithing is not a large group activity.

Parish Activity

What words or phrases best describe how the world would change
if your parish was successful in implementing its strategic plan?
Use these words to craft a vision statement.

8. Implement and Update

The seven steps just discussed can be accomplished in about three to four months, culminating in two planning sessions, about three hours each. The first session usually ends when you identify the three strategic issues. The second session concludes with the vision statement.

At the end of the second session, explain who is going to write up the results, how it will be edited, when it will be distributed to the rest of the planning committee, what will be the process for adoption, and when the plan should be ready to be communicated to the parish.

It never ceases to amaze me how many organizations spend hundreds of people hours in strategic planning but never implement the plan. A principle in community organizing suggests that "*anything worth planning is worth doing*—and *anything worth doing is worth evaluating*."

Once you have prepared, harnessed, and discerned the collective wisdom of the parish to determine what matters most, direct parish resources and focus parish attention on those issues.

Make your pastoral plan the focus of the *parish council*. The tendency is to breathe a sigh of relief, figure we got that done, and go back to business as usual. This is when leaders need to *create a sense of urgency about what is most important*. If we have decided that our strategic issues are the most critical issues facing the parish, they should dominate the agenda of our parish council, parish staff, and various commissions.

HOLD MEETINGS THAT MATTER.

Make sure that parish meetings focus on action. Keep reports to a minimum. Use a consent agenda. Expect people to read all reports before the meeting. At least once every three months, the parish council (which is usually the parish group most responsible for planning) should hold an accountability session to touch base, evaluate, and update the plan.

Go through every action step and ask for an update. Focus on the action items whose time has expired. Ask the person whose name is on those items to start the conversation. Ask, *How did we do on this item?* If it is finished, ask, *What is the next step to keep moving toward that strategy?* If it is not finished, ask, *Should we delete that item and replace it with something else? Should we change the item? Should we change the timeline?*

The key is to have a conversation about *each* action step. Update your action items. Then ask if any strategies need updating. If you have completed most of the original action items under a certain strategy, consider replacing that strategy. After a year or two, you might consider changing the strategic issues—or go through another pastoral planning process.

Strategic thinking is the ongoing work of strategic planning. Like a football coach that makes strategic adjustments when the wind changes or a key player gets hurt, pastoral leaders need to think strategically when changes occur or as progress unfolds.

Discussion Questions

1. Why are so many pastoral plans never implemented?
2. What can you do to increase the likelihood of implementation?

Strategy and Culture

Organizational culture is the sum of our attitudes, values, customs, beliefs, and behaviors. Culture is the *normal* way we do things. It is our patterns of behavior, our way of life.

Culture has a direct impact on strategy and vice versa. You cannot make real progress on a strategic issue, or the adaptive challenges associated with it, until you begin to change the culture. Many organizational change models identify culture as the last thing that changes.

People are more likely to *act themselves into a new way of thinking* than to think themselves into a new way of acting. If our strategic goal involves changing our collective way of acting, it will take more than tending to action steps on a pastoral plan to accomplish the change we wish to see.

ACT YOUR WAY INTO A NEW WAY OF THINKING.

Let's say your strategic issue is the following: *How can we become a more welcoming parish?* Some people think of welcoming as a ministry of greeters at Mass. That is a good start, but welcoming cannot stop at the front door. If we say our parishes are welcoming, then we need to establish welcoming at the core of our culture.

To be welcoming is to be open, friendly, and outgoing. This can begin at the front door, but are we open to new ideas among the people who we greet at the door? Do we welcome new ideas in our conversations and meetings? How often do we catch ourselves saying, hearing, or thinking, *We tried that before and it doesn't work!*

A *tacit assumption* is something we take for granted. An example of a tacit assumption is that our parish will always have a resident priest. Consider what happens when two to three parishes share a pastor. What happens when our tacit assumptions are challenged? How many tacit assumptions do we make about our parish? How hard is it when we are forced to face a new reality? How often do we try something new and innovative?

LEADING CULTURE INVOLVES TOP DOWN AND BOTTOM UP.

Cultural change happens from the *top down* and from the *bottom up*. Changing a tacit assumption or changing a cultural norm requires the work of those leading with and without authority. Cultural change is an opportunity for anyone to lead.

Let's say you want to change the culture about welcoming people at Mass. Any member of the parish can begin to change cultural norms with this simple step: Tell yourself that after each Mass, you will visit with at least one person you don't know before going to visit with your usual friends. After you have tried this for a few weeks, share your experience with others and ask them to join you. If they join you in this practice, you are leading. Together, you may change the culture to be more welcoming.

Action for cultural change can strike when the moment arises. Not all the steps taken toward cultural change can be listed in the pastoral plan. The steps in the pastoral plan should be a catalyst for other actions. Let's say I am having a conversation with a new parishioner in the coffee room. How I approach that person can make or break their feeling of being welcomed.

If we are to *act ourselves into a new culture*, we need to do more than change our pastoral plan. We need to change attitudes and behaviors whenever the opportunity presents itself. We need to change hearts and minds. That is the essence of leadership. That is why leadership needs to be diffused throughout a parish. We cannot rely only on those in authority to do the leading. They cannot be every-where.

THE STRATEGY CAN BE TO CHANGE THE CULTURE.

Culture is a major part of strategy. To act ourselves into a new way of thinking and being, we need to change not only our strategy but our culture as well. In fact, when addressing adaptive challenges, *the strategy can be the culture*.

Strategy and Structure

When Max Weber coined the term *bureaucracy*, he was studying the Catholic Church. He meant it as a positive term to describe how *larger organizations need to get smaller* by creating *bureaus*, which can be divisions or departments, to create order out of chaos.

A huge organization like the Catholic Church relies on *structure*. It clarifies who is in charge, who is responsible for what, and who reports to whom. Structure allows for good management. It can also enhance or impede leadership.

The problem develops when we don't breathe new life into our old structures. The old paradigm was command and control with authority. The new paradigm is to inspire, to invite, and to influence—with or without authority.

An unwieldy structure can suck the life right out of a parish. Think of multiple lines of approval to get things done. Structure can also create an illusion of control. We can establish rules that people figure are "meant to be broken." Structure can also create the expectation that authorities will control certain behaviors that they cannot control.

Control is about *extrinsic* motivation. Adaptive change requires *intrinsic* motivation.

Let's say the parish wants to change the behavior of some people leaving Mass after communion. Public edicts will be less effective than personal efforts. Try holding a private conversation with the people leaving early. You might even hear some interesting stories. And you might change some of the exit behavior.

THE STRATEGY CAN BE TO CHANGE THE STRUCTURE.

The most important change cannot be mandated. It often relies on *organic* leadership. Structures need to allow the rotation and emergence of leadership to occur.

Structure can dictate strategy. Strategy can dictate structure. Without structural support from the people in authority, a strategic plan will lack the resources or the attention to succeed. Without strategic support from the congregation, those in authority will not change the attitudes, behaviors, and values inherent in an adaptive challenge. When addressing adaptive challenges, *the strategy can be the structure.*

Reflection Questions

- What activities in your day would you describe as being *urgent but not important*?
- How can you eliminate some of these activities to make more time for matters that are *important but not necessarily urgent*?

Courage to Lead

Managers develop structure in our lives. Leaders breathe life into our structures. Remember that parishes need both leadership and management.

Why does the Church need leadership? For that matter, why does the world need leadership? Like any organization, the Church needs change. *Leaders ignite change.*

Without internal change to adjust to the external changes going on in our world, our organizations will die. This is the principle of *entropy*. If you are not growing, you are dying. If you are not changing, you are not growing.

Adaptive change will require courage from leaders and managers. *Courage* is the virtue that epitomizes the heart. To have courage is to "take heart." Jesus tells his disciples repeatedly to "not let your hearts be troubled" (John 14:27). He emboldens us with "do not be afraid" (Matt 14:27). Fear is the enemy of courage.

To lead change, you need passion for that change. Look into your heart. Find your passion. Connect with a sense of mission. What is it that you want to change? When you find that answer, your passion for the change will supply you with the *courage to lead*—as soon as those leadership moments present themselves.

As Pope Francis encourages us, "Remain steadfast in the journey of faith, with firm hope in the Lord.

This is the secret of our journey! He gives us the courage to swim against the tide. Pay attention, my young friends: to go against the current; this is good for the heart, but we need courage to swim against the tide. Jesus gives us this courage!"

Chapter Summary

In this chapter, we examined eight steps of *strategic planning* and applied them to create a model of *strategic pastoral planning*, which is based on discerning the future that God is calling us to. Strategic pastoral planning is a way to get everyone on the same page about what is *important* but not necessarily perceived as *urgent*. It begins with prayer and reflection on Scripture. It ponders our mission and helps us create a sense of shared vision.

The next chapter wraps up our study of pastoral leadership with its ultimate challenge: developing leaders to implement the pastoral plan. The best measure of servant leadership is not how many followers you lead. It's about how many leaders you develop.

References

Cox, Daniel, and Robert P. Jones. *America's Changing Religious Identity*. Public Policy Research Institute, September 6, 2017.

Drucker, Peter F. *Managing the Non-Profit Organization: Principles and Practices*. New York: CollinsBusiness, 1990.

Ebener, Dan R. *Servant Leadership Models for Your Parish*. Mahwah, NJ: Paulist Press, 2010.

Ebener, Dan R., and Frederick L. Smith. *Strategic Planning: An Interactive Process for Leaders*. Mahwah, NJ: Paulist Press, 2015.

Ganim, Carole, ed. *Shaping Catholic Parishes: Pastoral Leaders in the Twenty-First Century*. Chicago: Loyola Press, 2008.

Giving USA. *The Annual Report on Philanthropy for the Year 2016*. 2017. www.GivingUSA.com.

Grace, Kay S. *The Ultimate Board Member's Book*. Medfield, MA: Emerson and Church Publishers, 2009.

Heifetz, Ronald A., and Marty Linsky. *Leadership on the Line: Staying Alive through the Dangers of Leading*. Boston, MA: Harvard Business School Press, 2002.

Kotter, John P. *Leading Change*. Boston, MA: Harvard Business School Press, 1996.

——. *A Sense of Urgency*. Boston, MA: Harvard Business School Press, 2008.

Mogilka, Mark, and Kate Wiskus. *Pastoring Multiple Parishes: Emerging Models of Leadership*. Chicago, IL: Loyola Press, 2009.

Pope Francis. *Message for the Jubilee of Mercy to Young People*, January 14, 2016.

Schein, Edgar H. *Humble Inquiry: The Gentle Art of Asking Instead of Telling*. San Francisco: Berrett-Koehler, 2013.

Zech, Charles E., Mary L. Gautier, Mark Gray, Jonathon Wiggins, and Thomas Gaunt. *Catholic Parishes of the 21st Century: A Changing Church for a New Century*. New York: Oxford University Press, 2016.

Zech, Charles E., and Robert J. Miller. *Listening to the People of God: Closing, Rebuilding, and Revitalizing Parishes*. Mahwah, NJ: Paulist Press, 2008.

Chapter 6

Disciples and Apostles

Chapter 6 Preview

In this chapter we will explore the following:

- Why prayer and reflection become critical when leading a parish
- How leaders can develop a culture and structure that encourages leadership
- How *asking* instead of *telling* can encourage a culture of leadership
- How *leading with the right questions* can be an invitation to leadership
- What is *Humble Inquiry* (HI) and what is *Appreciative Inquiry* (AI)

St. Michael's Parish—Developing Leaders

Fr. Dave understood the importance of developing leaders from among the laity at St. Michael's. But at times, it was tempting to just do things himself. He was realizing that the temptations to use positional authority need to be kept in check every day.

While he recognized the need for change, it was very risky to lose control. What if the people started to change things not in the pastoral plan? Where could things go wrong? How was he supposed to be in charge if he had dozens of people practicing leadership? After all, wasn't he appointed by the bishop to bear the ultimate responsibility for the parish?

Yes, of course. The pastor is responsible to the bishop for the life of the parish. To that end, Fr. Dave had worked with his lay leaders to create a pastoral plan. The planning process had created a greater sense of shared commitment to the parish mission. It expressed a shared vision, but now it seemed like there was more work than ever to be done.

Once the pastoral plan is complete, the role of the pastor—and all parish leaders—is to focus attention on *inviting* even more people to lead the change as adopted by the parish. The key is to continuously call forth new leadership to keep the momentum moving forward.

In this chapter, we will discuss how best to inspire and encourage new leadership.

Daily Prayer

Sr. Gail Fitzpatrick gets up every morning at 3:30 to pray. Following the traditional Hours of the Divine Office as instituted by the Rule of St. Benedict, Sr. Gail stops to pray seven times every day, in addition to Daily Mass. During her day, she becomes very engaged in cooking, cleaning, gardening, sewing, or studying, but when the bell rings, she stops to pray.

"It is a joy and a blessing," Sr. Gail says. "Everything is wrapped around the Hours of the Office. It has become a part of me. I could not *not* say the Hours of the Office. It allows us to do what St. Paul says: To pray constantly. Without it, something is missing. It is part of the rhythm of life. It is very powerful, strengthening. The psalmody becomes a source of strength that pops up in your mind when you need it."

Sr. Gail is a member of Our Lady of the Mississippi (OLM) Abbey in Dubuque, Iowa, a community of religious women who belong to the Order of Cistercian of the Strict Observance. More than fifty years ago, she came to Iowa with twelve other nuns to establish the OLM community. She jokes, "All the other religious communities in Dubuque came by covered wagon. We came by jet plane," referring to a kind gentleman who lent his Learjet to fly the nuns to Iowa from Massachusetts in 1964.

"Prayer is my life blood," she says. "Once you get into the rhythm of prayer throughout the day, you become much more aware of everything else around you: the simple joys of living in community, the natural beauty of God's creation, and the activity of the Holy Spirit that moves in the stillness of silence."

When you meet Sr. Gail, you can sense that she has spent her life centered in prayer and meditation. She has a presence of quiet strength and humility. She speaks from a well-formed heart and a well-trained mind. She reminds me of the words of St. Paul, who bids us to take on the "mind of Christ" (1 Cor 2:16; see also Phil 2:5–8).

PRAYER PRIMES US FOR LEADERSHIP.

Athletes, actors, and musicians train for hours each day. How many hours do we spend training to become *missionary disciples*? How do we prepare ourselves for *visionary apostleship*? How do we tend to the health of our hearts, minds, and spirits?

Experience shows that time spent in prayer, meditation, and scriptural reflection prepares our hearts and minds for the challenges of leadership. Opportunities for prayer and reflection are already there. We simply have to seize the moment.

Research shows that we live happier and healthier lives when we become more empathetic in our hearts and more attentive in our minds (Begley). When we begin our meetings with prayer, even a perfunctory prayer if read with meaning and intentionality, we remind ourselves of our purpose, our reason for being.

Training for Leadership

We don't become fit by joining a fitness center. We don't become religious by joining a religion. We don't become a leader by reading this leadership book. It takes training and practice. Being more conscious of where we focus our attention, more mindful of our emotions, and more aware of the effect that our behavior is having on others must become a daily practice (Rom 12:2).

Christ calls us to be renewed in mind, body, and spirit (Rom 8). As we discussed earlier, preparation for leadership is an *inside-out* process. Daily prayer, reading of Scripture, and reflection on our experiences must become routine. As Mother Teresa taught, all of life becomes part of our spiritual lives. Prayer is not separated from the daily grind of life.

Even as we become *apostles* for Christ, we must constantly remain *disciples* of Christ. To practice leadership, we need to be human beings fully capable of leadership. That means a daily focus on our own emotional, spiritual, and personal development. Apostles for Christ continue to be disciples of Christ.

Remember that disciples are *called* (Matt 4:19) and apostles are *sent* (Matt 28:19). Disciples become apostles—just as followers become leaders: students become teachers, stewards become evangelists, and passive members of a parish can become active agents for change.

This is the cycle of Christian life and liturgy: At the beginning of the liturgy, we are welcomed as *disciples*, members and stewards. By the end of that liturgy, we are invited to go out as *apostles*, leaders and evangelists, to love, serve, and change the world.

As Sherry Weddell points out, the charism of *pastoring* is not limited to those who are *canonical* pastors. You must be ordained to be the canonical pastor. To be a *pastoral leader*, you just need to find your burn. Discover your passion. Let it burn into your consciousness like a candle that illumines your mind and heart. Connect your passion to your parish mission: To what change is God calling you and your parish? How can you enable more people to encounter Christ in their lives?

Open your heart, your mind, and your will to receive guidance from the Holy Spirit (Rom 8). Discern the direction that God is calling you personally (Rom 12:2). Enter into a dialogue with other members of your parish to discern where God is calling you collectively. Align your will with God's will for you and your parish.

At some point, you will discover that the change you want to see is *too big for one person* to lead. You will find that what you really need is not more followers but *more leaders*. Leaders lead change. The activity of leadership can be practiced by any person who influences others to join them in a change effort. When you come to this realization, the next step in practicing leadership is to develop the leadership capacity of others.

Calling Forth Leaders

You may have heard it said, "We have too many chiefs but not enough 'Indians.'" This common verse holds two myths, one about "Indian chiefs" and the other about "Indians."

First, Native American chiefs are among the best examples of servant leadership. They have a legacy of putting themselves at the service of the tribe for its protection and preservation. Decision-making among indigenous tribes provides some of the best examples of reaching consensus. Decisions are made by the tribal council, with consultation but not dictation from the chief.

The world could use more, not less, of these types of *chiefs*—those who are willing to place themselves at the service of the whole tribe.

PERHAPS WE HAVE TOO MANY HEAD HONCHOS AND NOT ENOUGH LEADERS.

Second, the verse seems to suggest that what we really need is fewer people in authority and more people to follow the directives of those in authority. Just as we mischaracterize Native American chiefs, so too we misunderstand the role of the tribe. In a dialogue among Native Americans, leadership can rotate from one person to the next. The voice of every person in the circle is important and consulted.

This is the practice of *dialogical leadership*. Followers are engaged and willing to rotate in and out of leadership roles. Those in authority encourage this rotation.

THE REAL CHALLENGE OF LEADERSHIP IS NOT HOW MANY FOLLOWERS YOU CAN LEAD,
BUT HOW MANY LEADERS YOU CAN DEVELOP.

Leaders Can Emerge Anytime, by Anyone, Anywhere

Consider the following story told by a student at St. Ambrose College in the 1950s. The students were waiting for the professor, talking about how long they should wait before leaving. Meanwhile, a janitor was outside mopping the hall, listening to the chatter. One student made the smart aleck remark that maybe the janitor could deliver the lecture. Everyone laughed.

But then came the surprise. The janitor did just that. He walked up to the podium, and the student recalls that "what he said was so memorable that many of us later said it was the most important lecture we heard in our college years." The student recounts what he said:

> When you invited me to speak, I know it was a joke, but I do have something to say.
> When I was young, I did not have the money to go to college. Instead I went to work
> to support my family. I work hard, do a good job, and value what I do, but my work will
> never take me to the heights as what you can reach, provided that you do not waste
> your chances and appreciate what has been given to you. That's my message to you.

At that, he smiled, turned, left the podium, and returned to his work. You could have heard a pin drop. No one moved, and fifteen minutes had by now come and gone. First a trickle, then a sincere burst of applause, filled the hall. The student now says, "It was the most memorable lecture of my years at St. Ambrose. I often think of that janitor, that day and that most valuable lesson" (McDaniel).

In my own school years, I was influenced by many support staff. I can recall bus drivers, janitors, and school secretaries who made an impact on my life. One of my students tells a story about a teacher's aide who changed the culture of the whole school around "bus duty." Most school staff dread bus duty. It requires greeting students off the bus and accompanying them to the classroom. However, this aide brought a great deal of positive energy and enthusiasm to the role. The whole school noticed how the children were much more prepared to learn.

She serves as another example of how followers can become leaders, and how leadership can emerge from anywhere. However, it is more likely to emerge when the culture supports new leadership. It is a Catch-22 dilemma. We need to change our culture so that more leadership can emerge *to further*

---

change our culture. Those in positions of authority play a key role here. They can create incentives for change or they can be a disincentive for change.

When Sam O'Donnell fixed the front door of St. Michael's, he did not have to get permission from his pastor. This type of freedom is more likely to occur in a smaller parish, where there are fewer committees or hired help to work around.

The simple structure allows for more initiative. Sam was not stepping on someone else's toes as he fixed the door—as he might in a larger church or in a parish with a different culture.

Clearly, the culture that Fr. Dave created at St. Michael's affirmed the initiative that Sam took. Sam knew he had the support of his pastor. That support creates a culture that can enable parishioners like Sam to move from disciple to apostle.

The culture of a small parish is more likely to encourage the people to treat the parish like a home. If something is broke, you fix it. You can take action without multiple layers of approval. The adaptive challenge in larger parishes, as with all large organizations, is this:

As we get bigger, how can we get smaller?

The use of small groups is essential. People can get lost in a large parish. They need the structure to allow for one-on-one relationship building. The structure and the culture of the parish can encourage or discourage lay engagement, active participation, and especially the development of leadership.

Pope Francis has indicated that structural and cultural change is a priority for the Church. He has called for less authoritarianism and more lay participation in decision-making, less bureaucracy and more dialogue about organizational structures, and less secrecy and more transparency in the business dealings of the Church.

The less authoritarian the culture, and the simpler the structure, the more likely new leaders will step up, take the initiative, and lead. Those in authority might assume they are supposed to be in control, have all the answers, and get all the credit. Status and promotions are too often associated with being in control, having the answers, and getting the credit.

LEADERSHIP IS ABOUT ASKING.

Edgar Schein says we live in a "culture of do and tell." Let's consider how the culture of our parishes might change if we took on a different approach. What might happen if we led by *asking* instead of *telling*? How might that encourage more leadership to emerge?

Leading with Questions

True story: A man approaches his boss on a Friday and tells him, "I've got to take off work on Monday." The boss responds by telling him, "There is no way you can get off on Monday. I've got three people taking off that day already." The worker swears at his boss. The boss swears back.

The worker goes down the hall and files a complaint with his union, stating that (a) his boss would not let him take Monday off, even though his wife was having major surgery that day, and (b) he swore at him. Technically, the worker was right on both counts.

Imagine how different this story would have gone if both parties (or either party) had used asking instead of telling. The worker asks, "John, is there any way I can have off on Monday?" John replies, "Hey, Tom, what is happening on Monday?" (Note that both parties in this version of the conversation start with a question.)

Tom replies, "Well, I just found out my wife is having major surgery on Monday and I need to be with her." John replies, "Well, I've already got three people taking off on Monday, but hey, Tom, I'll cover your shift for you myself."

In this case, the simple act of *asking instead of telling* could change the whole dynamics of the meeting. In the real-life case, it could have prevented a union grievance that led to conflict mediation for the whole department.

When we are in a position of authority, or we want to impress people with how much we know, we tend to be more assertive in telling and less cooperative in listening. That is the nature of living in a culture of do and tell. However, if we want to get the best version of the other people around us, we will find that it is much wiser to ask and to listen.

Jesus was famous for asking questions. According to the count by Martin Copenhaver, in the four Gospels, Jesus asks 308 questions! Some of his most memorable quotes are not statements but questions: "Who do you say that I am?" (Matt 16:15); "What do you want me to do for you?" (Mark 10:51); "Where is your faith?" (Luke 8:25); "Why do you worry?" (Matt 6:28); "Do you love me?" (John 21:17); and "What are you looking for?" (John 1:38).

JESUS ASKED 308 QUESTIONS.

Jesus seems more likely to ask questions than to provide answers. In fact, he is asked 183 questions and only answers 3 times with a direct answer (Copenhaver). Many of Jesus' parables are told in response to questions. For example, the story of the Good Samaritan is his reply to the question, "Who is my neighbor?" (Luke 10:25–37).

When St. Paul first encounters Jesus, he comes in the form of a question: "Saul, Saul, why do you persecute me?" (Acts 9:4).

Jesus asks questions to inspire, clarify, persuade, confront, confuse, and disarm, according to Copenhaver. Jesus challenges the notion that leaders must have all the answers. In fact, he seems to be the one with all the questions.

Michael Marquardt suggests that asking instead of telling is one way to build *social capital*, which equates to higher levels of trust, commitment, and cohesion. He states, "Leaders, through questions, can build a culture in which questions are welcomed, assumptions are challenged and new ways to solve problems are explored."

Asking questions can nurture a culture where everyone is on a search for a higher level of truth. It encourages those who have something to contribute but have never been asked. Unfortunately, too many parishioners are waiting to be asked. They hesitate to volunteer their time, their talent, or their ideas until and unless someone asks them.

Let's say you are a member of a parish council. Part of your job is to find and develop your replacement. Get to know people personally: *What are their gifts and talents? What are their strengths? What are their interests?* Then invite them to contribute accordingly. Invite them to take initiative. Be on a continuous talent search.

Once you discover that talent, set up a time when you can visit more personally with them. Approach them with humility and curiosity as you ask these questions: *What matters most to you? How would you like to see this parish improve? How can we approach a certain problem in this parish as an opportunity? What are some options for improvement? How can you help?*

Humble Inquiry

Bishop Daniel Flores was visiting with a brand-new employee, asking questions to see how her new job was going. As diocesan receptionist, she described her work as "answering the phone, figuring out who can help, and connecting them." The bishop responded, "Sounds exactly like my job." What a humble way for a bishop to 1.3 million Catholics to relate to someone who was already intimidated by his stature.

The bishop was practicing *Humble Inquiry* (HI). It is about asking questions for which you don't already know the answers. You ask questions with genuine curiosity and interest in the other person. You act as if that other person is your teacher and you are there to learn.

The word *humility* comes from the same root word as *humanity*, which means "from the earth." To be humble is to be down to earth, to be grounded in the reality of what is means to be fully human, recognizing both your strengths and your weaknesses.

HUMBLE INQUIRY IS DRIVEN BY HUMILITY, CURIOSITY, AND EMPATHY.

Humility teaches that the more we know, the more we realize we don't know. To lead with questions requires (a) the *wisdom* to know what we don't know, (b) the *humility* to admit that to others, and (c) the *courage* to act accordingly.

Humble Inquiry is a way of finding out what others think, instead of telling others what we think. Increasingly, in this complex and fast-moving world, we need to find out what others think. We need the input of others to make decisions.

Let's say that a surgeon is about to operate on the wrong patient, or the wrong shoulder. If no one in the room is willing to speak out, the result can be disastrous. The person in authority who demonstrates humility will build confidence in others to know that they can speak out, especially when he is making a mistake.

Admitting mistakes is a sign of strength, not weakness. Mistakes show that we are *human*, which is the essence of humility. To be humble is to recognize fully our human strengths as well as our human weaknesses. Humility honors the roots of our humanity, so we can develop the wings of our leadership.

TO BE HUMBLE IS TO BE FULLY HUMAN.

To be *humble*, per the sower and the seed (Matt 13:1–23), is to get your hands dirty. It is to dig into the thoughts and ideas of others instead of digging further into your own positional thinking. Humble Inquiry is the art of asking questions that open the other person to share things you don't know. It is searching for the best possible solution rather than convincing people that you are right.

Let's say your parish council has decided that evangelization is one of its strategic issues. You want to start conversations about this with members of the parish. You could ask, "What are the best ways to grow membership in our parish?" "How can we reach out to the Nones?" "How is God calling you to help grow this parish?"

Asking these types of question is the first step in HI. Then you listen. The next question should emerge out of the conversation (not rehearsed in advance). Lock into what the other person is saying. Be truly curious. Resist the temptation to tell. Ask questions that will help you gain their perspective without tainting their idea with yours.

Parish growth is an adaptive challenge for which there is *no easy answer*. If you approach people with the humility that suggests you do not have the answers and the curiosity that suggests you really want to know what the other person thinks, these questions can open up a fascinating dialogue. They can demonstrate that you are open to other people stepping up to share their ideas.

Practicing Humble Inquiry can encourage people to step up and lead.

Parish Activity

Select an intriguing topic, for example: What would you most like to change in this parish? Pair up one-on-one and practice Humble Inquiry. For greater fun, tape the interaction and get together with your partner to watch and evaluate yourselves.

Ask Open Questions

Once you open the conversation with a humble question, stay inside the conversation. Ask *open-ended* questions such as *how* and *why*. They encourage the other person to open up. Demonstrate that you are following along, probing into their thoughts and feelings, summarizing their ideas, and helping them to think adaptively. Try not to change the subject or ask leading, loaded, or closed-ended questions that suggest a solution or steer the person toward what you think the other person should think, do, or say.

LEADERS ASK THE RIGHT QUESTIONS.

Humility means being open to the possibility of being wrong. *Inquiry* means being open to what the other person is saying.

Advocacy is the opposite of inquiry. It means convincing others that we are right. The questions we ask can easily slip into advocacy if we ask *leading* or *loaded* questions, such as "Don't you think we ought to change the music in our Mass?" That is a statement disguised as a question. It is neither humble nor inquiring.

Some questions are asked to focus on our point of interest or to steer the conversation in *our* direction. Other questions can state our ideas put in the form of a question. We ask some questions to fit our narrative or to shift the focus toward our interest.

Closed questions are *either-or* questions. They seek a specific answer to a specific situation, such as "When is our next meeting?" or "What is on the agenda?" They can be used to clarify and confront but not to inspire dialogue. They usually are more relevant to technical solutions, whereas open questions are more relevant to an adaptive challenge.

With the challenging issues we face as a Catholic Church, we could ask open questions like the following: *Why are our attendance numbers declining? Why have the numbers been rising for other churches? How do they do it? What can we learn from this? What can we do differently?* Sherry Weddell adds the question, "Where is God in all of this for you?"

Questions should not drive our preconceived notions of solutions. When we come into a meeting with a hidden agenda, delivering a forceful or charismatic speech, we cannot expect to create a *shared* vision or build consensus.

HUMILITY BEGETS OPENNESS.

Let's say that someone makes a mistake. Let's say the boss responds, "How could you possibly think that this was the best way to handle the situation?" Technically, this is a question. But the answer is assumed in the question. It is an *accusatory* question, one that expects the other person to admit that they were wrong, and they should have handled it differently. The person being asked is probably just going to say they are sorry or do whatever they can to get out of trouble. This type of question is neither humble nor inquiring.

Consider if, in the same situation, the person asks an open question like, "Why did you decide to handle the situation in that manner?" Just a slight change, but this invites a conversation about the mistake that was made. Both people are more likely to learn something with this approach. It presents both sides with the opportunity to teach and to learn what different options may have been better. Either way, the relationship would grow between the two because the leader showed that person respect, and that person will be more likely open to change and more willing to communicate with the leader in the future.

Leading with questions is an art and a science.

The *art* is to be truly humble about your own shortcomings and curious about the views of the other person. Shed your own preconceived notions that you must be the one with the right answer or the best solution. Place yourself totally at the service of the group. That is more likely to harness the wisdom of the group.

The *science* is using the right prompts: (1) open-ended questions that invite the other person to take the conversation in their own direction; (2) encouraging responses that indicate interest and attention; (3) summaries that instill confidence that you are listening; and (4) clarifying questions that help you understand.

HUMBLE INQUIRY CAN CHANGE THE CULTURE.

Just as important as what you include in your communication toolbox is what you *exclude*: your thoughts, judgments, and opinions. The tendency when first practicing HI is to respond with your viewpoint or to test whether the other person agrees with your solutions. Your job is to listen and to understand, not to test whether the other person agrees with your ideas.

Leading with questions creates a welcoming atmosphere of openness and respect. When the people in positions of authority in a parish are asking instead of telling, it can change the culture of a parish. It can encourage more people to step up and lead.

Ask, Then Listen

Once we ask the right questions, we listen. As Edgar Schein explains it,

---

1. Listen to the words and the emotions behind the words.

2. Demonstrate that you understand by summarizing and reflecting.

3. Show that you care by empathizing.

Some call this *intentional listening*. Others call it *active listening*. Otto Scharmer uses the phrase *generative listening*, which means to open our ears, our hearts, our minds, and our will to the potential to change.

To listen is to tune into someone else and to consider the path they have taken. It helps us connect with others. It builds relationships. It shows we care. It opens the door for an honest exchange. It also raises the *receptivity* of the other person to listen to what we want to say.

> As the saying goes:
> People don't *care* how much you know…
> until they *know* how much you care.

Given the rapid pace of change in our world today, we tend to speed up everything around us, including our conversations. We do not allow enough time for the single-minded listening that ensures good, honest, and effective communication. The irony is that we waste time when we do not get the message right the first time and need to go back to fix our mistakes.

TO PREPARE FOR A MEETING, TRY TO THINK ABOUT WHAT YOU ARE GOING TO HEAR.

Let's say you are heading into a big meeting. Do you prepare for that meeting by rehearsing what you are going to *say*? Or do you think about what others might be thinking? What if we spent more time reflecting on *their* needs and interests? The tendency is to plot our way to convince others to meet *our* needs and interests. We could reflect on how their ideas and interests might be *compatible* if not *complementary* with our ideas and interests. We could ask ourselves in advance, *How can we both get what we really want and need?*

Listening is opening oneself up to be influenced by others. It allows the other person to lead. By listening, we show interest in the ideas of others. If we want new leaders to emerge, we need to listen. This includes being willing to hear critical or constructive feedback about what we are doing—without becoming defensive or taking it personally.

Humble Inquiry affirms the other person. It encourages others to speak up and present their viewpoints. It builds a culture of *ask and listen* instead of *do and tell*. Generally speaking, when someone asks you a question, and the issue is *adaptive* in nature, your first instinct should be to ask, "What do you think?"

When their question is *technical* in nature, and you know the answer, it is better to tell than to ask. For example, if you know how to use the copy machine, and someone asks you for directions, you don't ask, "Well, how do you think it works?"

On the other hand, if the other person has already learned how to use the copy machine, and you insist on telling her how to use it anyway, it can be very demotivating. When you tell people how to do a job they already know, it feels like *micromanagement*. This can be a death knell for initiative, engagement, and emergent leadership.

Delegation

The opposite of micromanagement is *delegation*. Delegation is not dumping. It is not a way to clear your desk of tasks you don't want to do. It is not about making certain tasks just go away. Delegation is conducted with (1) *support* and (2) *feedback*. You ask the person to check in with you on a regular basis and let you know if they need any help. You make sure they have the resources they need to make sure they succeed.

Delegation can be a means of developing leadership in others. Delegate jobs that are important to the parish—not the ones you want to dump. Find a good fit between the needs of the parish and the gifts and talents of the new leader. Practice HI to find out how it is going, what they need, and how you can help.

When Bishop Martin Amos asked me to conduct leadership training for young priests in the Diocese of Davenport, he wanted me to emphasize the need for delegation. He explained that when a pastor tries to do everything by himself, he (1) takes away leadership opportunities from other members of the parish and (2) wears himself out.

DELEGATION IS NOT DUMPING. IT REQUIRES FEEDBACK AND SUPPORT.

This is precisely the sound advice that Jethro gave to his son-in-law, Moses, when he came to visit him (Exod 18). Moses was working from morning until night, dispensing with the judgments for the Jewish people. He took his responsibilities very seriously and thought he was doing the right thing. He wanted the people to understand and respect the law.

Jethro observed all this and essentially told Moses that he was micromanaging every decision by making sure every judgment went through him. He was creating a bottle neck, with long lines of people waiting for his judicial decisions. Jethro told Moses that he was wearing out himself and the people. He suggested that Moses delegate some of the responsibility to lower level judges, which is what Moses did.

JETHRO TAUGHT MOSES ABOUT DELEGATION.

The tendency is to do things by ourselves instead of spreading the work around. Doing something by myself does give me more control of the work. However, it limits the amount of work that can be done, and it limits the number of people who can feel a part of the work.

Bishop Daniel Flores told this story about delegation to his leaders in the Diocese of Brownsville: When God sent the angel Gabriel to make the announcement to Zechariah (Luke 1:11–20), God demonstrated the art of delegating instead of doing things himself. Perhaps, the bishop suggested, that is why God asks *us* to do the work of evangelization and stewardship, faith formation, and social justice.

Bishop Flores suggested that perhaps it is the very nature of God to work through others instead of doing things himself. God doesn't snap his fingers and make things happen. He works through all of us. To lead like God, we should ask others to get involved in our work, instead of trying to do everything ourselves. We should ask others to take leadership on certain initiatives instead of trying to lead all the change.

Ask yourself these questions: *What fulfills your life? What gives you* flow? *What makes your heart sing? What is your sweet spot, your passion?* Find ways to focus your energies in that direction.

Ask others the same questions. Consider using programs like *Strength Finders* or *Called and Gifted*

---

to identify people's strengths, gifts, and charisms. Then feed people the roles they will thrive in, rather than dumping the projects you don't want. Delegate responsibilities that fit their strengths, gifts, and charisms.

Also ask yourself, *What draws the life right out of you?* Find someone to help with that part of your work. Delegate some of that responsibility—but do it with support and feedback. Find a good balance between what you *want* to do and what you *have* to do. Hold the essential reins of your position but not every single detail. Find the right fit, considering your strengths and those of others on your team.

Appreciative Inquiry

Humble Inquiry can be your *entre* into *Appreciative Inquiry* (AI). This is a communication approach that builds on the strengths of an organization rather than trying to fix weaknesses (Cooperider). It explores new ideas and dares to dream new realities. It creates an openness for change and sets out to cocreate a new vision through meaningful dialogue.

Appreciative Inquiry assumes that change occurs when we change the questions we ask, such as the following: *What is good about this parish? What are we doing well? What are you most interested in? How can this parish grow? How can we develop new leaders? How can you help?* The response to these questions can create positive energy for change. It inspires positive action to make that change.

Like HI, AI requires mindfulness and presence to focus on what is possible. It requires asking and then listening. It invites us to look positively at the *past* as we project a positive image on the *future*. It begins with a focus on living in the *present* moment as we listen with intention.

Live in the Present Moment

Paul exhorts us to *direct our thoughts* to Christ (Phil 4:8), *put on the mind* of Christ (1 Cor 2:16), and *keep our attention* carefully fixed on Christ (2 Pet 1:19).

Like Sr. Gail, we all need to set aside time for prayer and reflection. We can "awaken our eyes each day with the light that comes from God and our ears to His voice which cries to us daily from Heaven" (Rule of St. Benedict; see also Rom 13:11).

One way to focus on this light is to reflect each night on three things we are grateful for. By counting our blessings during our bedtime prayers, we program our brain to focus on what is positive. This fosters spiritual growth and literally feeds the neurological pathways that create a more optimistic outlook in our brains.

PRAYER INSTRUCTS US TO LIVE MORE FULLY IN THE PRESENT MOMENT.

A basketball player who is thinking about his postgame remarks in the fourth quarter might see the ball slip through his hands at a key moment, drastically changing what he is going to say in that postgame interview.

One meeting gone awry can make it hard to focus on the next meeting. If you have someone come into your office and share some news that shakes you to your core, such as asking you to plan their funeral, or telling you they are going to quit, it is hard to focus on the story of the next person who walks into your office.

As leaders, we can train our minds to think about what we want to think about. We can refuse to wander into thoughts of the past or the future when we are supposed to be listening to the person right in front of us. We can focus our attention on the present whether we are sitting in a classroom, listening at a meeting, or worshipping at Mass. Some people can walk through the woods and hardly notice the wonders of nature all around them because they are so absorbed in their thoughts.

When meeting with another person, it is critical that we practice the conscious, purposeful, and intentional practice of being attentive to what is happening right now. The neuroplasticity of our brain means the brain is always open to new growth. It allows us to improve attention by practicing mindfulness. This can cause brain reorganization, where we reshape the habits of our brain through our daily practices—for better or worse.

Let's say, for example, you are trying to turn your full attention to what is taking place during the Mass. Because the liturgy is so familiar to us, it is easy to wander off. When that happens, it is important to shift our attention back to the purpose of the Mass. This is what *Sacrosanctum Concilium* called "fully active and conscious participation."

FOCUSING OUR ATTENTION DURING MASS STRENGTHENS OUR HEARTS AND MINDS.

As my colleague Frank Agnoli puts it, active participation by the laity during Mass is accomplished even during the silence of listening to the homily. Frank says that when we practice active participation in the liturgy, our worldviews are challenged, and we begin to see connections between Scripture, theology, and our daily lives.

When we are very intentional about keeping our attention on the Mass, we strengthen the pathways in our brain in ways that will help us maintain our attention in other aspects of life. Such mindful practice will pay off when we need to listen attentively to someone later in the day. It can help us pay attention to the facial expressions of a fellow parishioner who is upset. When we are attentive, we are restructuring the neural connections in our brains. Using our minds, we make conscious choices about what we are going to pay attention to.

Sometimes it is helpful to take a few moments in the parking lot and remember why you are attending a parish council meeting or going to Mass. Find a quiet space to center yourself. Put aside what just happened (the past) and what is going to happen (the future) so you can concentrate on living in the present moment.

Hear the words of the Mass like they are brand new. As the Rule of St. Benedict suggests, *Sing in such a way that your mind is in harmony with your voice.*

Focus on what someone else is saying in each and every moment. This type of practice will enrich your experience of going to Mass, saying the rosary, or interacting with others.

Reflect on Your Listening Skills

When we foster reflection, we become more self-aware. We also become more socially aware. We learn to appreciate the views of others. We identify with what they are saying and feeling. We begin to see Christ in the other person.

LISTENING IS A VIRTUOUS ACT.

Imagine that your last parish meeting was videotaped, and you are watching yourself in interaction with others. To reflect on the quality of your listening, ask yourself *active* questions, not passive ones. Instead of asking what was happening to you or what others were doing to you, ask what you were doing to others:

	How actively did I listen?
	How did I demonstrate that I was listening?
	Did I summarize what they were saying?
	Did I reflect the emotions behind the words?
Ask yourself	Did I talk over anyone or cut them off?
	Did I shut out distractions?
	Did I listen with my heart, my mind, and my will?
	Or did I listen to respond, to judge, or to debate?
	Can I find Christ in the other person?

The Virtues of Listening

Listening requires the following:

- *Wisdom* to realize we don't have all the answers
- *Humility* to admit that to others
- *Empathy* to move out of self and identify with the other person
- *Patience* to endure the pain of someone else's burdens
- *Mercy* to act on what we learn

Chapter Summary

In this chapter, we discussed how leading with questions, practicing Humble Inquiry and Appreciative Inquiry, and listening to each other can create a culture that encourages pastoral leadership. We reminded ourselves that persistent prayer and reflection on Scripture help us to be fully active, conscious, and present to those we are trying to lead.

Closing Prayer

Let me conclude with a prayer:

Open my spirit, Lord...that I may discern your will.

Open my mind, Lord...that I may reflect on your ways not mine.

Open my ears, Lord...that I may listen more carefully.

Open my eyes, Lord...that I may see more clearly.

Open my heart, Lord...that I may feel with empathy.

Open my hands, Lord...that I might reach out to help.

Open my will, Lord...that I might change my ways into your ways.

Open my eyes and ears, my mind and heart, my hands and my will, Lord...so that I can become a more active disciple and a more willing apostle.

References

Begley, Sharon. *Train Your Mind, Change Your Brain: How a New Science Reveals Our Extraordinary Potential to Transform Ourselves*. New York: Ballantine Books, 2007.

Bohm, David. *On Dialogue*. New York: Routledge, 1996.

Cooperider, David L., and Diana Whitney. *Appreciative Inquiry: A Positive Revolution in Change*. San Francisco: Berrett-Koehler, 2005.

Copenhaver, Martin B. *Jesus Is the Question: The 307 Questions Jesus Asked and the 3 He Answered*. Nashville: Abingdon Press, 2014.

Lefton, Robert E., and Victor R. Buzzotta. *Leadership through People Skills*. New York: McGraw-Hill, 2004.

Marquardt, Michael J. *Leading with Questions: How Leaders Find the Right Solutions by Knowing What to Ask*. San Francisco: Jossey-Bass, 2014.

McDaniel, Fr. George. "Spirit Messages for St. Ambrose University," 2017.

Mother Teresa. *A Simple Path*. New York: Ballantine Books, 1995.

Pope Francis. *The Joy of the Gospel (Evangelii Gaudium)*. Rome: Libreria Editrice Vaticana, 2013.

Scharmer, Otto, and Katrin Kaufer. *Leading from the Emerging Future: From Ego-System to Eco-System Economies; Applying Theory U to Transforming Business, Society, and Self*. San Francisco: Berrett-Koehler Publishers, 2013.

Schein, Edgar H. *Humble Inquiry: The Gentle Art of Asking Instead of Telling*. San Francisco: Berrett-Koehler, 2013.

Conclusion

Love, Truth, and Beauty

"Blessed are those who hunger and thirst for righteousness, for they will be filled."
—Matthew 5:6

The Beatitudes provide us with eight mighty views of the kingdom, which is our vision, our inspiration, our home (Matt 5:1–12). We catch glimpses of the kingdom when we are most in need of God. The Beatitudes can send us homeward bound to the kingdom.

The first four Beatitudes teach us that we can experience God's blessing when we encounter some human form of suffering (Matt 5:3–6). The source of their blessing is to be poor in spirit, mourning, meek, or hungry for righteousness. The second four Beatitudes are more action based (Matt 5:7–10). The source of their blessing is to be merciful, pure of heart, a peacemaker, or persecuted for righteousness. God blesses all who live by these Beatitudes.

HUNGER FOR CHANGE DRIVES HUNGER FOR LEADERSHIP.

The fourth Beatitude (Matt 5:6, see above) speaks of hunger for what is righteous, that is, what is right and just. Hunger was the source of one of Jesus' temptations in the desert (Matt 4:3). To be hungry is to be human. To receive the food of God's kingdom is divine. In each of these Beatitudes, Jesus weaves pearls of wisdom into a beautiful portrait of the kingdom.

Many people hunger for renewal and change in the Church. We need more young families involved, more dedicated stewardship, more compassionate outreach to the poor, and more active engagement from a wider group of leaders and members.

Leading with Love, Truth, and Beauty

Aquinas suggests that God influences human activity not with coercive power but through his love, truth, and beauty. These are the three primary spheres of human activity. The Greeks called this the Good, the True, and the Beautiful. Aristotle taught that humans are motivated by *logos* (reason—our heads), *pathos* (emotion—our hearts), and *ethos* (personal experience—our hands).

GOD IS LOVE. GOD IS TRUTH. GOD IS BEAUTY.

One of the most memorable phrases of the Vatican II conference was the call for the "fully conscious and active participation" of the laity in the liturgy. This means not only will laypeople be involved with their hearts and heads during the service but also with their hands when they live out the Mass by loving and serving the Lord.

Leaders need to appeal to the faithful at all three levels—the head, the heart, and the hands. In a homily, the preacher includes elements that appeal to the Truth revealed in Scripture (*the head*), the Love that God expresses for us (*the heart*), and the Beauty of the beloved community, which can only be built when we change our attitudes and behaviors (*the hands*).

Leading with Authority

Distinguishing leadership from authority does not diminish the need for authority. It simply creates another way of thinking about leadership. We can lead with or without authority. Working in hierarchical structures or authoritarian cultures may make it harder to lead because the standard is to control and to dictate. Of course, change can be dictated from the top or from the outside. But this is not leadership.

You can order a change in behavior by creating a new policy or establishing a new rule. It might be a new parish or diocesan policy. It might be necessary for the good of the community. The problem with dictating change is that you get less buy-in and more resistance. The challenge of leadership is to find more persuasive and less coercive ways to enact change.

Without change, there is no leadership. If you are not changing something, you are not leading. But dictating change is not leadership. Leadership is not coercive. Remember our definition: Leadership must be *voluntary* and *interactive*. If you are bullying people to get what you want, that makes you a bully, not a leader.

The Church is a *voluntary* organization. People can use free will to leave the Church. They can get up and walk out on their pastor or leave their parish whenever they want. Look around the world: Numbers are down for church attendance. Weddings and baptisms are down in most places. Funerals are up. We are losing members faster than we are replacing them.

We tend to train people in technical skills but not people skills. When people reach a certain level of experience, we promote them into positions of authority. Seminaries train priests who are expected to perform as pastors. Universities create teachers who are promoted to be deans or principals. Boot camp produces privates but not generals. Scanning the landscape of leadership, we see the greatest need is for people skills, not technical ones.

ALL CHANGE DOES NOT REQUIRE LEADERSHIP, BUT ALL LEADERSHIP REQUIRES CHANGE.

The work of leadership we have described here assumes and requires that the people in authority are *patient, merciful, and humble*. These are the three qualities that Pope Francis identified as the most important for leadership. To force your will upon others is neither patient, merciful, nor humble. Forceful actions will discourage others from participation. People will be less likely to take the initiative on projects they might be passionate about.

Leaders who have a position of authority can make the switch from an authority relationship to a relationship based on mutual influence. Leadership is worth the risk. Leading instead of ruling will further the cause of your mission.

TO LEAD WITH AUTHORITY, YOU MUST RESIST THE TEMPTATION TO USE THAT AUTHORITY.

The key to leading with authority is to resist the temptation to rely too heavily on your positional authority. Leading with authority requires that you set aside that authority. To lead when you have authority, lead as if you did not have that authority.

Paradoxically, leading with authority is influencing without using your authority.

Leading without Authority

Remember that we are all called by the Great Invitation to be *disciples*, who are followers of Christ. We are also called to respond to the Great Commission to be *apostles*, who are leaders for Christ. Disciples become apostles just as followers become leaders.

TO LEAD WITHOUT AUTHORITY, YOU MUST RESIST THE TEMPTATION TO GO WITH THE FLOW.

Leaders *without* authority have more leverage. As volunteers, they can decide to leave their ministry if they get frustrated. In the same way that people in the workforce are more likely to leave their bosses than their jobs, people in parishes are more likely to leave their pastors than their ministry. Some will quit; others will find another place to do ministry.

As Paul advised the Corinthians, "Keep alert, stand firm in your faith, be courageous, be strong" (1 Cor 16:13). As St. Augustine pointed out, the Church is not just a hotel for saints but a hospital for sinners. As my friend Don Mosley puts it, "All the darkness in the world cannot put out the light of one candle" (see John 1:5).

We need patience as we learn how to influence with and without authority.

Without leadership, there is no change. The Church needs change. Therefore, we need more leadership—and less command and control authority.

We need the type of leadership that intrinsically motivates people to want to be involved, to be fully engaged. We cannot order the Nones to go to church. We cannot force the fallen away Catholics back to church. Nor can we command the less active Catholics into fully active, conscious participation and engagement.

We need to invite, inspire, and influence people in *loving, truthful, and beautiful* ways.

"Finally, beloved, whatever is true, whatever is honorable, whatever is just, whatever is pure, whatever is pleasing, whatever is commendable, if there is any excellence and if there is anything worthy of praise, think about these things" (Phil 4:8).

References

Blake, Robert R., and Jane S. Mouton. *The Managerial Grid*. Houston: Gulf Publishing, 1964.

Ebener, Dan R. *Blessings for Leaders: Leadership Wisdom from the Beatitudes*. Collegeville, MN: Liturgical Press, 2012.

Forest, Jim. *Ladder of the Beatitudes*. Maryknoll, NY: Orbis Books, 1999.

Pope Francis. *The Joy of the Gospel (Evangelii Gaudium)*. Rome: Rome: Libreria Editrice Vaticana, 2013.

Second Vatican Council. Constitution on the Sacred Liturgy (*Sacrosanctum Concilium*). Rome: Libreria Editrice Vaticana, 1963.

Appendix A

Focus Interview Guide

From *Strategic Planning: An Interactive Process for Leaders*, by Dan R. Ebener and Frederick L. Smith (Mahwah, NJ: Paulist Press, 2015).

Our Focus Interview Guide

1. What are your general impressions about this organization?

2. What are the strengths of the organization?

3. What are the weaknesses of the organization?

4. What are some improvements that can be made to the organization?

5. What should the organization stop doing (if anything)?

6. Where are opportunities for growth?

7. What threats are there to the organization?

8. List strategies for moving forward.

9. Final thoughts or comments.

Appendix B

Lectio Divina Shared in Community[1]

Fr. Luke Dysinger, OSB
St. Andrew's Abbey, Valyermo, California

(A) Listening for the Gentle Touch of Christ the Word

(*The Literal Sense*)

1. One person reads aloud (twice) the passage of Scripture, as others are attentive to some segment that is especially meaningful to them.

2. **Silence** for 1–2 minutes. Each hears and silently repeats a word or phrase that attracts.

3. Sharing aloud: (A word or phrase that has attracted each person.) A simple statement of one or a few words. **No elaboration**.

(B) How Christ the Word Speaks to Me

(*The Allegorical Sense*)

4. Second reading of same passage by another person.

5. **Silence** for 2–3 minutes. Reflect on "Where does the content of this reading touch my life today?"

6. Sharing aloud: **Briefly**: "I hear, I see…"

(C) What Christ the Word Invites Me to Do

(*The Moral Sense*)

7. Third reading by still another person.

8. **Silence** for 2–3 minutes. Reflect on "I believe that God wants me to _____ today/this week."

9. Sharing aloud: At somewhat greater length, the results of each one's reflection. (Be especially aware of what is shared by the person to your right.)

10. After full sharing, pray for the person to your right.

Note: Anyone may "pass" at any time. If instead of sharing with the group you prefer to pray silently, simply state this aloud and conclude your silent prayer with ***Amen***.

---

1. Note: The author, Fr. Luke Dysinger, OSB, considers the material in this appendix to be in the public domain. It may therefore be downloaded, reproduced, and distributed without special permission from the author. It was first published in the Spring 1990 (vol. 1, no. 1) edition of *Valyermo Benedictine*.

Glossary

Accommodation—Surrendering or agreeing with the other party without being assertive

Adaptive challenges—Issues for which there are no easy answers or technical solutions

Adaptive leadership—Leadership that addresses adaptive challenges (see above)

Amygdala—The front sections of the limbic system responsible for fear and anger responses

Apostles—Greek for "sent forth," Latin for "messenger," or to be leaders for Jesus

Appreciative Inquiry (AI)—A process of questioning that affirms the best in people

Assertive—Expressing yourself with neither passivity nor hostility

Attunement—Old English for "to bring into harmony," to tune into emotions of another

Authority—Latin for "originator," the formal power that comes from a position

Beatitudes—Latin for "blessings," opening eight lines of the Sermon on the Mount

Behaviors—Pattern of action taken by a person, what they do

Brain—The physical center of the emotional, intellectual, and nervous system

Called and Gifted—A program for discerning people's gifts, talents, and charisms

Character—Greek for "distinctive mark," the fruits of practicing virtue

Charisma—Greek for "gift from God," or in English, attraction toward another

Charismatic leadership—Leadership based on charisma of the presumed "leader"

Closed question—Question that can be answered with one specific answer, for example, yes or no

Collaboration—Latin for "work together," integrating the needs and interests of both parties

Coercive power—Ability to fire, discipline, and make decisions that force others to comply

Competition—Latin for "strive for," rivalry to fight for your own needs and interests

Concept mapping—Activity where group is asked to draw a picture of an abstract concept

Consensus—Latin for "agreement," one that everyone can live with

Consent agenda—Agreement to approve all written reports in one motion

Consultative hierarchy—Structure of authority where dialogue is encouraged

Conversation Cafes—Activity that allows small groups to contribute to multiple conversations

Culture—Latin for "to cultivate," values, customs, and beliefs of an organization or a country

Debate—Latin for "to batter," a discussion where both parties intend to compete and win

Deflect—To respond to a question by asking others what they think

Delegation—Latin for "to commission," to pass a responsibility (with support and feedback)

Dialogue—Greek for "to gather together," or "to speak through," a conversation

Dignity—Latin for "worthy"; in Catholic thought, it is based on being created by God

Disciples—Greek for "called forth," Latin for "to learn," or to be followers of Jesus

Emotional intelligence (EI)—Self-awareness, self-control, social awareness, and social guidance

Emotional quotient (EQ)—A measure of emotional intelligence (EI)

Emotions—Latin for "to move," your physiological reaction to an event

Empathy—Greek for "feeling" or "passion," the ability to share the emotions of another

Engagement—An emotional commitment to an organization and its mission and goals

Extrinsic motivation—Latin for "outward," rewards or punishments

Feeling—The meaning that you attach to an emotion, based on your cognitive interpretation

Followers—Those who are actively involved in leadership, often being trained for leadership

Generative dialogue—Conversation that models generative listening (see below)

Generative listening—Listening with an open mind, open heart, and open will

Humble Inquiry (HI)—A process of asking questions with humility, empathy, and curiosity

Humility—Greek for "earthly," being fully aware of human strengths and weaknesses

Inquiry—Latin for "to seek within," the process of asking questions

Inspiration—Latin for "to breathe within," to motivate the "spirit"

Intrinsic motivation—Latin for "inward," to be moved by the mind, spirit, or heart

Kenosis—Greek for "to empty" yourself of selfish desires, that is, to take on the mind of Christ

Leadership—Voluntary, interactive process that produces adaptive change

Leading question—Question that poses the suggested answer within the question

Limbic system—The emotional center of the brain

Loaded question—Question that assumes the worst in the person being questioned

Management—Positional authority with administrative responsibility for certain operations

Micromanagement—Controlling the actions of subordinates down to every little detail

Mind—Conscious awareness that interprets and can control what is happening in the brain

Mindfulness—Being fully alert, conscious, or aware, living fully in the present moment

Mission—Your bottom-line purpose, your reason for being, the social benefit you provide

Narcissism—Greek for "self-love," or in English, arrogance

Neuroplasticity—The ability of the brain to change and grow

Neuroscientists—Those who study the brain

Nones—Those who do not identify themselves with any specific religion or denomination

Open question—Question that opens the other person to discussing whatever they want

Organizational citizenship—A person's voluntary commitment to an organization

Pastoral planning—Parish planning based on discerning the will of God

Plus/Delta—Quick way to evaluate your meetings, based on pluses and minuses

Power—Latin for "to be able," the ability to act

Proprioception—Latin for "own reception"; it includes the ability to think about your thoughts

Prosocial behavior—Positive actions that build social capital (see below)

Receptivity—Latin for "to receive," the level of openness, readiness to listen

Referent power—Ability to influence based on character and reputation

Reflective probe—Calling an emotion by name during a dialogue

Relationship conflict—Disagreements that escalate into people problems

Relationship of leadership—The trust, commitment, and cohesion within the team

Respect—Latin for "to look again," to recognize the dignity of the other person

Robert's Rules of Order—Rigid set of parliamentary rules governing decision-making

Self-awareness—Ability to be aware of your own emotions

Self-control—Ability to guide your own behavior, especially during an emotional episode

Servant leadership—Leadership based on a motivation to serve

Shared vision—Common goal or vision that is created by the whole team

Social awareness—Ability to identify with the emotions of others

Social capital—The measure of relationships on a team, including trust, loyalty, and cohesion

Social guidance—Ability to handle gracefully the emotions of others

Social intelligence—Social awareness plus ability to act with grace in emotional situations

Strategic—Greek for "general's view of the battlefield," a comprehensive overview

Strategic issue—Critical, comprehensive, changeable problem facing an organization

Strategic pastoral planning—Incorporating strategic planning into pastoral planning

Strategy—Possible solution to a strategic issue

Strengths Finders—A program for identifying people's strengths

Structure—Latin for "to build," arrangement of systems, departments, or divisions

Subordinate—Latin for "inferior rank," or "less than ordinary," those of a lower position

Summaries—Shortened version of what the other person is saying

Task conflict—Disagreement about the task itself, for example, the solution to a problem

Task of leadership—The strategy, the goal, or the change you wish to see

Technical solution—Applying what is already known to fix a problem

Traits—Characteristics or qualities that describe a person

Transformational leadership—Leadership based on intrinsic motivators

Virtue—Latin for "moral perfection," a trait that helps achieve lasting joy or happiness

Vision—Latin for "to see," the picture of success, the future direction of your organization

Wisdom—Greek for "knowledge," plus learning plus experience

Index